# GermEval 2024 Shared Task on Statement Segmentation in Germany Easy Language (StaGE)



Vienna, Austria
13 September 2024

ISBN: 979-8-3313-0486-7

**Printed from e-media with permission by:**

Curran Associates, Inc.
57 Morehouse Lane
Red Hook, NY 12571

CURRAN ASSOCIATES INC.
proceedings
.com

**Some format issues inherent in the e-media version may also appear in this print version.**



Association for Computational Linguistics
209 N. Eighth Street
Stroudsburg, Pennsylvania 18360

Phone: 1-570-476-8006
Fax: 1-570-476-0860

acl@aclweb.org

**Additional copies of this publication are available from:**

Curran Associates, Inc.
57 Morehouse Lane
Red Hook, NY 12571 USA
Phone: 845-758-0400
Fax: 845-758-2633
Email: curran@proceedings.com
Web: www.proceedings.com

# Proceedings of GermEval 2024 Shared Task on Statement Segmentation in German Easy Language (*StaGE*)

**co-hosted at the 20th Conference on Natural Language Processing KONVENS 2024**

University of Vienna
September 13, 2024

# Preface

German Easy Language (Leichte Sprache) is a controlled, simple language for which there have been several guidelines in the past. The draft of DIN SPEC 33429 has the potential to become the authoritative guideline. It describes several characteristics of German Easy language. Two of these are the number of statements and to format enumerations as lists. We have, therefore, segmented Easy Language sentences and annotated how well these aspects of DIN SPEC 33429 are implemented in web texts in German Easy language.

Based on this, we present one of the GermEval 2021 Shared Task on Statement Segmentation in German Easy Language (StaGE). GermEval 2024 part of a series of Shared Tasks on processing German that was started in 2014. The shared task is co-located with the Conference on Natural Language Processing (KONVENS), which is held in Vienna in 2024. The results and the full dataset can be found at the shared task website at https://german-easy-to-read.github.io/statements/. We are grateful to all participants whose high-quality contribution made GermEval 2022 a great success. Furthermore, we want to thank the KONVENS 2024 conference organizers and the GSCL.

Vienna, September 2024
The organizing committee

## Organizers:

Thorben Schomacker (Hamburg University of Applied Sciences)
Miriam Anschütz (Technical University of Munich)
Regina Stodden (Heinrich Heine University Düsseldorf)

# Table of Contents

## Workshop Program

| | |
|---|---|
| 10:00 – 10:15 | Opening |
| 10:15 – 11:15 | Keynote by Christina Niklaus from University of St. Gallen |
| 11:15 – 11:30 | Overview of the GermEval 2024 Shared Task on Statement Segmentation in German Easy Language (StaGE) |
| 11:30 – 11:45 | KlarTextCoders at StaGE: Automatic Statement Annotations for German Easy Language |
| 11:45 – 12:00 | Statement Segmentation for German Easy Language Using BERT and Dependency Parsing |
| 12:00 – 12:35 | Brainstorming for possible next (shared) tasks |
| 12:30 – 12:45 | Closing & group photo |
| 12:45 – 15:00 | Lunch |

# Overview of the GermEval 2024 Shared Task on Statement Segmentation in German Easy Language (*StaGE*)

**Thorben Schomacker**[1*] , **Miriam Anschütz**[2 *] , **Regina Stodden**[3 *] ,
**Georg Groh**[2], and **Marina Tropmann-Frick**[1]
[1]Hamburg University of Applied Sciences
[2]Technical University of Munich
[3]Heinrich-Heine University Düsseldorf
statements@soc.cit.tum.de

## Abstract

Sentences in easy language should only contain a few statements to enhance their readability. However, there exists no common definition of statements or tools that could automatically extract them. With this shared task, we try to close this gap in German Easy Language. We drafted a set of annotation guidelines and created a dataset with manually extracted numbers of statements and statement spans. We attracted three participating teams that tried to automatize the annotation process to automatically annotate the statements. All submissions are based on a BERT classification system and could outperform our naive baselines. However, especially the statement span extraction is challenging and requires further research. Our shared task tries to facilitate and motivate further research in this direction.

## 1 Introduction

In recent years, a growing community of researchers in computer science and computational linguistics has been working on facilitating writing in German Easy or Plain Language by providing machine learning models and corpora for training or evaluating them, e.g., Säuberli et al. (2020); Deilen et al. (2023); Madina et al. (2023); Jablotschkin et al. (2024) as well as for other languages (Alva-Manchego et al., 2020; Štajner et al., 2023).

German Easy Language (DE: "Leichte Sprache", also called "easy-to-read language") is a controlled language, which increases accessibility and comprehensibility (Bredel and Maaß, 2016). This language is, for example, characterized by using simple and short words, avoiding complex sentence structures (e.g., passive voice, nominal style, or conjunctive mood), and minimizing the statements per sentence. Besides other easy-to-read standards (e.g., Bredel and Maaß 2016 or Netzwerk Leichte Sprache 2022), the DIN SPEC 33429 (DIN-Normenausschuss Ergonomie, 2023) defines the characteristics of the German Easy Language. While currently only available as a draft version, it has the potential to become the ruling guideline in the future.

However, the evaluation of whether a (automatically or manually) generated text is readable and suitable for the target group is still a big challenge (Stajner, 2021; Cumbicus-Pineda et al., 2021). The characteristics or list of requirements for German Easy Language texts are often not considered in the evaluation process. Currently, either the target group is asked whether they face issues with the text (Stajner, 2021) or metrics are used to automatically estimate the texts' simplicity, fluency, and meaning preservation (Alva-Manchego et al., 2020) or all of the aspects at once (Maddela et al., 2023).

In order to integrate the German Easy Language characteristics into the evaluation process more, we are following a modular approach per characteristic respectively. In this work, the characteristic of our interest is the number of statements. At this time, there is only a limited amount of literature available and no practical implementation to solve the above problem. For example, the DIN SPEC 33429 does not further define "one statement". To scientifically operationalize the guidelines, we aim at closing this gap. Therefore, we introduce the "GermEval 2024 Shared Task 2: Statement in German Easy Language (StaGE)"[1] to ignite a scientific debate on how to segment and identify statements in German Easy Language. Our contributions can be summarized as follows:

*Equal contribution. Order determined by coin flip.

[1]https://german-easy-to-read.github.io/statements/

1. We provide an annotation guideline on the identification and segmentation of statements in German sentences.

2. We release a gold standard dataset including manual annotations regarding the number and segments of statements in German Easy Language sentences.

3. We organized a shared task that introduced the first approaches regarding the automatic identification and segmentation of statements in German Easy Language sentences.

In the following, we introduce the shared task in more detail and provide an overview of the shared task's results. Our data, evaluation method, and baselines are publicly available for further experiments.[2]

## 2 Related Work

This shared task contributes in a three-fold manner:

### 2.1 Corpora

In recent years, many text simplification corpora have been introduced which include German Easy Language, e.g., Simple German Web Corpus '13 (Klaper et al., 2013), GEASY corpus (Hansen-Schirra et al., 2021), Simple German Web Corpus '23 (Toborek et al., 2023), MILS corpus (Schomacker et al., 2023), DEplain-web corpus (Stodden et al., 2023), DE-Lite corpus (Jablotschkin et al., 2024) as well as web harvesters that download texts in German Easy Language from the web, e.g., Klepp (2022), or Anschütz et al. (2023). Most of these corpora include professionally simplified texts, e.g., news texts (see NDR Nachrichten[3], MDR Nachrichten[4]) or texts of public authorities (see Stadt Hamburg[5] or Stadt Köln[6]). But, the web harvester also includes texts written by non-professional translators, i.e., articles of `hurraki.de`.

[2] https://github.com/german-easy-to-read/statements

[3] https://www.ndr.de/fernsehen/barrierefreie_angebote/leichte_sprache/Nachrichten-in-Leichter-Sprache,nachrichtenleichtesprache100.html

[4] https://www.mdr.de/nachrichten-leicht/nachrichten-in-leichter-sprache-114.html

[5] https://www.hamburg.de/barrierefrei/leichte-sprache

[6] https://www.stadt-koeln.de/service/leichte-sprache/index.html

Most of the corpora listed above do not contain other linguistic annotation. One exception is the LeiKo corpus (Jablotschkin and Zinsmeister, 2021) in which the authors annotated colon construction in simplified and Standard German. Some sentences of the DEplain-web corpus (Stodden et al., 2023) are also annotated with simplification operations including structural changes, e.g., rewriting from passive-to-active voice, reordering, or splitting. Furthermore, the APA-RST corpus (Hewett, 2023) includes a structural analysis of the texts, but they are written for foreign language learners and not the target group of German Easy Language.

For English, there is the MinWikiSplit corpus (Niklaus et al., 2019b) and the BiSECT corpus that focuses on syntactic simplification. The MinWikiSplit corpus contains 203,000 complex-simple sentence pairs where the simplified parts are automatically segmented into minimal meaningful propositions using the TS framework DISSIM (Niklaus et al., 2019a). The BiSECT corpus (Kim et al., 2021) includes English simplification pairs where a complex sentence is either split into two simple sentences, or two complex sentences are merged into one simple sentence. Another BiSECT version exists with German simplification pairs, but they have major encoding problems (i.e., all diacritical markers are missing).

Nevertheless, we are not aware of a high-quality German corpus including syntactic simplification or any other kind of annotations regarding the number of statements in Easy Language texts.

### 2.2 German Text Simplification Approaches

Most existing German text simplification systems focus on generating texts for foreign language learners (e.g., Säuberli et al. 2020 or Spring et al. 2021), for laypeople (e.g., Trienes et al. 2022), for a mixed group (e.g., Ryan et al. 2023, Klöser et al. 2024 or Fruth et al. 2024), but only a few address the German Easy Language target group (e.g., Siegel et al. 2019 or Deilen et al. 2023).[7] However, due to the lack of corpora for syntactical German simplification, there are no German text simplification systems that focus on syntactic simplification.

But, we are aware of English TS systems that bring syntactic and semantic separation into focus that are related to our approach of statement segmentation. DISSIM (Niklaus et al., 2019a) aims at

[7] For a more detailed overview, we refer to Madina et al. (2023) or Stodden (2024).

splitting English sentences into "minimal propositions" based on hand-crafted rules. Niklaus et al. define minimal propositions as utterances that cannot be further split into meaningful propositions and that represent a minimal semantic unit. In comparison, Jamelot et al. (2024) aim at separating so-called "rheses" in French and English texts. Rheses are also defined as small and syntactically meaningful units of a sentence but are additionally based on the prosody of the text. Their system is intended to split the segments based on syntactic dependency trees, punctuation marks, and prosodic features. Our annotation procedure of "statements" is closer to the definition of minimal propositions than rheses.

### 2.3 Evaluation of simplified texts

Evaluating the quality of simplified texts is a hard task to solve, which is rooted in the challenge of defining a standard simplified output. Grabar and Saggion (2022) name two reasons behind this root challenge: (1) it is not factual since it relies on transformations, and (2) it is heavily based on the own knowledge and opinion of people and thereby not consensual. Furthermore, unlike for standard language, a *native simplified-language speaker does not exist* (Siddharthan, 2014). There have been several attempts to solve this challenge:

Deilen (2020) analyzed eye-tracking data collected from people with impairments to investigate the effects of certain simplified language stylistics, such as separating longer nouns via a hyphen. Säuberli et al. (2024) conducted a survey of people with and without cognitive impairment using various questionnaires to measure the comprehensibility of the texts. Cumbicus-Pineda et al. (2021) proposed a checklist-based evaluation, but each of the items is verified manually. In contrast, in the automatic evaluation of text simplification, the focus is on measuring simplicity, fluency, and meaning preservation (Alva-Manchego et al., 2020). But, neither of these aspects considers characteristics of Easy (German) Language. Evaluations based on existing guidelines for simplified language have not yet been implemented but have been theorized (Schomacker et al., 2024; Madina et al., 2024).

### 2.4 Shared Tasks

Recent shared tasks in the scope of German text simplification have focused on the level of lexical simplification. For example, the identification of complex words in sentences (Yimam et al., 2018), the prediction of the complexity of German sentences for foreign language learners (Mohtaj et al., 2022) or the prediction of the complexity of a word within a German sentence and the suggestion of a simpler synonym (Shardlow et al., 2024). To the best of our knowledge, there is no shared task that focuses on syntactic simplification of German.

## 3 Task Description

The goal of the shared task is to identify the number of statements and the statement spans in the sentence. We do not aim to force authors to write one-statement sentences exclusively but rather make the current statement distribution per sentence transparent to them. In addition, we allow authors to re-think their texts and re-phrase them to increase readability with reference to German Easy Language guidelines.

### 3.1 Sub Tasks

The shared task consists of two subtasks and the participants can submit their systems to both of the tasks independently. In subtask 1, we only estimate the number of statements that are present in the sample. For the second subtask, the respective statement spans are annotated. Figure 1 shows how our annotated data looks line. The two subtasks refer to two separate columns. In the first column, we only state the number of statements in the sentence, which corresponds to subtask 1. For the second subtask, we tackle the statement spans as distinct sets of words. For the example in Figure 1, the sentence "Diese Flugzeuge transportierten Nahrung und Brenn-material." (*These planes carried food and fuel.*) contains two statements: "The planes carried food" and "The planes carried fuel". There are two different things carried by the planes that the readers have to understand. Even though they might be related, they are two separate chunks of information that the readers have to digest.

### 3.2 Use Cases

We envision the following use cases for statement and statement span annotations:

**Complexity assessment** as part of a holistic German Easy Language assessment (Mohtaj et al., 2022). German E2R gives clear rules about the number of statements in sentences. Therefore, the assessments can be utilized for editorial purposes or direct feedback for writers.

| Phrase_tokenized | #Statements | Statement spans |
|---|---|---|
| 0:=Diese 1:=Flugzeuge 2:=transportierten 3:=Nahrung 4:=und 5:=Brenn-material. | 2 | [ [3] , [5] ] |

Figure 1: Example Annotations from our trial data set. We enumerate the tokens in the sentence to simplify referring to them in the statement span annotations. In this case, we annotate the tokens that belong to the different spans as a set of statements spans. For more information on the annotation process, refer to Appendix A in the Appendix. Our data is open source and can be downloaded on our homepage.

**Rule-based simplification** is actively researched for German (Suter et al., 2016) and could also profit from incorporating statements. Using discourse-aware statement splits, a similar approach achieved promising results for the English language (Niklaus et al., 2019a).

**Statement-aware evaluation** could increase the performance of overlap-based metrics like BLEU (Papineni et al., 2002) and ROUGE (Lin, 2004). A similar metric is described and implemented in Sulem et al. (2018).

**Fact checking** of statements as atomic facts. The extracted statements can be considered atomic facts and checked individually for truthfulness. This statement-wise evaluation facilitates the detection of partially-correct information (Min et al., 2023).

## 4 Data Set and Evaluation

### 4.1 Data Set

Our corpus contains texts from the Hurraki wiki site, a German online dictionary. We used the scraper by Anschütz et al. (2023) and scraped the articles as of January 2024. The texts are supposed to be written in German Easy Language by people who are not obligatorily trained in writing in this controlled language. The texts are not verified before publication, and thus, they may contain errors such as punctuation or grammatical errors. However, we do not correct any typos manually, but if the errors are severe, e.g., if two sentences are merged into one due to missing punctuations, these samples are manually annotated as erroneous.

In terms of pre-processing, we have split the texts into sentences at punctuation marks, and hence, they can span over several lines. The tokens in the sentence are separated by white spaces and consecutively numbered (see *Phrase_tokenized* in Figure 1). A statement only contains full tokens; we don't split tokens for sub-token annotations. If a sentence spans several lines (as typical for LS), the line breaks are displayed with `\newline`.

Figure 1 exemplifies a data sample from our trial dataset. We manually annotated the sentences regarding the number of statements contained in them (see *#Statements* column). The distinct statements of a sentence are annotated at the word level (see *Statement spans* column).

#### 4.1.1 Annotation Guideline

Our annotation process consists of two parts: the statement splitting and the annotation of the statement spans. To determine the number of statements, we split the sentences at conjunctions. Additional pieces of information like adjectives, adverbs, or prepositional constructions form separate statements. The detailed rules for statement splitting are explained in Appendix A. If a statement does not include a verb or if it contains multiple sentences, we annotate it as 0 statements to indicate it is erroneous. However, we do not include samples with 0 statements in our test and eval splits.

For the statement span annotations, we enumerated the tokens in the sentence in ascending order. With this, we could easily refer to them in the statement span annotations. The statement spans are only annotated for samples with more than 1 statement. We annotate the tokens that belong to the different spans as a set of statements spans. In addition, we define the following rules:

- The order of the spans and the order of tokens within the spans is not important and can be altered.
- Articles, coordinating conjunctions, and "\newline" are never included in the spans. In contrast, subordinating conjunctions, relative pronouns, or filler words are included.
- Only the mutually exclusive parts are annotated, i.e., tokens that are contained in all statements are not annotated.

Example annotations can be found in Figure 1 and Table 6 in the Appendix.

For the annotation process itself, we split the full dataset into chunks of around 500 samples. Articles should be complete and should not span over multiple chunks, and thus, the chunks vary in size. For each chunk, two of the authors annotated the data independently. If the two annotators agreed on their annotation, we kept it for the final dataset. Otherwise, if the two annotators disagreed, we showed the samples to a third annotator who chose the correct annotation. We had three different annotators. All annotators are German native speakers and have experience with German Easy Language. The inter-annotator agreements range from 64.38% to 73.21%. Overall, we annotated 4,553 samples in 9 chunks and removed erroneous and ambiguous samples. Then, we split the data into train (2,944 samples), test (416 samples), and final evaluation (878 samples) splits. For the test and evaluation sets, we additionally removed the 0-statement samples.

#### 4.1.2 Data Structure

In Hurraki, articles consist of three different elements. The first element is the short abstract that contains the most relevant information about the topic. The second element is a picture, and the last element is a more detailed description with further information. Hurraki provides metadata for their articles, such as the article's category or the timestamp of the last edit. We kept this metadata to construct a rich dataset. In addition, we pseudonymized the author to enable analyses of differences in writing styles among different authors. Table 1 gives an overview of the information available in our dataset.

#### 4.1.3 Statistics

The basis of the task is a dataset (Figure 2) consisting of over 4000 entries, and it is available with an open license[8]. We have included sentences with 0 statements in the train data, which means that those sentences are incomplete or erroneous. In this case, even sentences with multiple statements can be annotated by 0. Nonetheless, we left them in the data to create real-world experiences but removed them from the test and eval datasets. Furthermore, we achieved a similar distribution of 1-statement sentences (52%, 62%, 50%), which formed the largest class of sentences in each of the three sub-dataset. This distribution similarity was only achieved for 2-,3- and 4-statement sentences. Since 5- and 6-statement sentences are very rare and could almost be considered outliers, their distribution differed across the sub-datasets.

| Column name | Description |
|---|---|
| **topic** | Defined by the lower-case title of the Hurraki article title. |
| **phrase** | Original phrase. |
| **phrase_ number** | Number of the phrase. "_long" indicates, that the phrase belongs to the detailed explanation |
| **genre** | Genre(s) extracted based on Hurraki's categories |
| **timestamp** | Time of the article's last modification. |
| **phrase_ tokenized** | Phrase separated in tokens. Each token is given an index for referencing. |
| **num_ statements** | Number of statements. |
| **statement_ spans** | List of statements. Each statement is a span of words, represented by their indices. |
| **author** | Pseudonymized (md5-hash) author id |
| **notes** | Optional notes by the annotators. |

Table 1: Column names and description of the available information in our dataset.

### 4.2 Evaluation

We evaluate the two subtasks independently and use different metrics for each of the subtasks. Our evaluation scripts are published so that the performances of future systems can be reported easily[9].

#### 4.2.1 Subtask 1: Number of Statements

The first task is a classification problem where the participants should determine the number of statements in the sentence.

**F1-Score** For this classification problem, we evaluate the submissions according to precision, recall, and F1-score. As our data is heavily unbalanced,

[8] https://github.com/german-easy-to-read/statements/tree/master/data

[9] https://github.com/german-easy-to-read/statements/tree/master/data/scoring

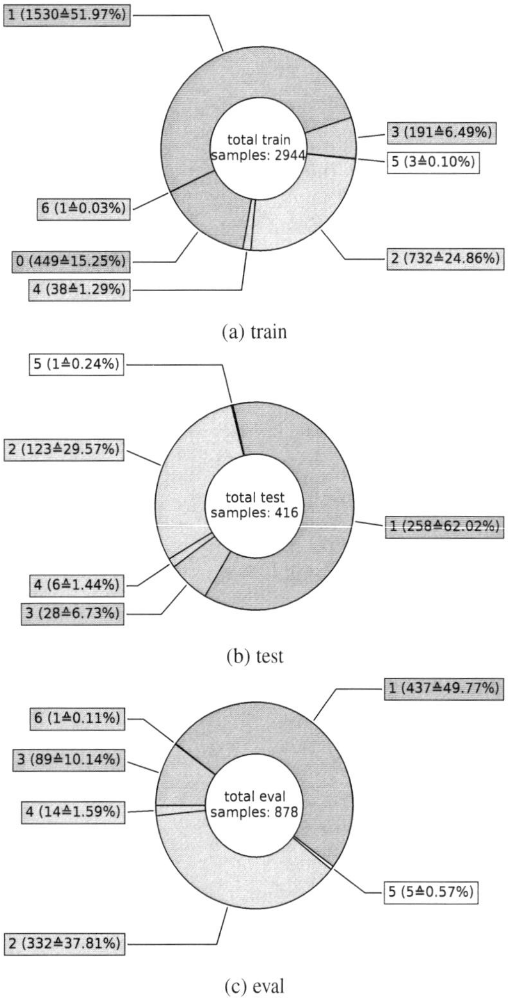


Figure 2: Distribution of the number of statements per sentence in the train, test, and eval datasets.

we averaged the F1-scores between the different classes by weighting the number of samples in the respective class.

**MAE & MSE** However, this evaluation judges all mispredictions equally and does account for less severe off-by-one errors. Therefore, we add an evaluation on a continuous scale, which is the mean absolute error (MAE) and the mean squared error (MSE). We considered the MAE as the most meaningful and, thus, ranked the submissions based on this metric.

#### 4.2.2 Subtask 2: Segmentation of Statements

The evaluation of subtask 2 is more complex. If we only rewarded exact matches, the scores would be very low and could not account for almost correct annotations. Therefore, we selected chrF, which evaluates the spans based on character n-gram overlaps, and the Jaccard index, which interprets the annotations as sets and measures the overlap with the ground truth.

**chrF** (Popović, 2015) is designed as a machine translation evaluation metric that measures the F1-score of n-gram character overlaps between the candidate and the reference translation. For our evaluation setup, we interpret the statement spans as string sequences and calculate the overlap between the proposed statement spans and the reference annotation. For samples with more than ten tokens, the corresponding indices contain two digits that would be interpreted as separate characters during evaluation. Therefore, we replaced all numbers by single letter characters and thus obtained an equal weighting of all indexes. In addition, we sorted the spans in an ascending order to avoid lower scores due to the index order.

For the score calculation, we use the standardized implementation of the sacrebleu package (Post, 2018). We ignored whitespaces and set the character n-gram order to 6 and the word n-gram order to 0.

**Jaccard** index, or the Jaccard similarity coefficient, is a statistical mean used for gauging the similarity and diversity of sample sets. We adapted it, so that it is applicable for a list of sets. We iterate over all sets in the gold truth $Y$ (with length=$N$) and the sets in the prediction $\hat{Y}$ (with a variable length) to calculate the Jaccard index for each of the tuples, which summed up to build the $J_{list}$ score. To increase the robustness, we sort the sets by min, max, and median value and average the different $J_{list}$-values.

$$J_{list}(Y, \hat{Y}) = \sum_{n}^{N} J(y_n, \hat{y}_n) \quad (1)$$

$$J(A, B) = \frac{|A \cap B|}{|A \cup B|} \quad (2)$$

Note that by design, $0 \leq J(A, B) \leq 1$. If A intersection B is empty, then $J(A, B) = 0$.

## 5 Results

Three different teams participated in our shared task. While two teams submitted predictions for both subtasks, one team only submitted their system to subtask 1. The results can be seen in Table 2 for task 1 and Table 3 for task 2. All teams outperformed our baselines for both tasks. When comparing the predictions with a paired t-test against the all-1 baseline, all systems, but also our string-match baseline, achieve statistically significant improvements[10].

| Team | MAE↓ |
|---|---|
| KlarTextCoder | 0.35 |
| StaGE FriGHt | 0.40 |
| CUET_Big_O | 0.40 |
| Baseline: string-match | 0.60 |
| Baseline: all-1 | 0.65 |
| Baseline: random | 0.92 |

Table 2: Results Final Phase – Subtask 1

| Team | chrF↑ | jaccard↑ |
|---|---|---|
| KlarTextCoder | 0.36 | 0.29 |
| StaGE FriGHt | 0.30 | 0.38 |
| CUET_Big_O | - | - |
| Baseline: random | 0.24 | 0.27 |
| Baseline: string-match | 0.05 | 0.04 |
| Baseline: all-1 | 0.00 | 0.00 |

Table 3: Results Final Phase – Subtask 2

### 5.1 Baselines

We provide three baselines to rank and evaluate the participant submissions. The first baseline assumes that all phrases only have one statement. Since single statement samples are the most common in our data (see Figure 2), this baseline can be seen as a majority voting system. According to our task design, we only annotate the statement spans if the number of statements in the sample is greater than one. Therefore, all statement spans are empty for this baseline.

The second baseline is a random baseline that randomly assigns a number between one and three to the number of statements. If there are at least two statements, we split the sample into the corresponding number of statement spans at random indices. The spans must be non-empty, and we split them into equal or near-equal sizes.

[10]P-values are $1.6e^{-12}$ for the string-match baseline, $9.8e^{-119}$ for CUET_Big_O, $9.16e^{-64}$ for StaGE FriGHt, and $1.1e^{-97}$ for KlarTextCoder.

The first rule of our annotation guidelines (Appendix A) separates statements via conjunctions. Our third baseline considers this rule and counts the occurrences of the conjunctions "und"(*and*), "oder"(*or*), and "aber"(*but*). In addition, the statement spans are determined by splitting at these conjunctions without annotating the conjunctions themselves.

### 5.2 Proposed Systems

**KlarTextCoder** (Ramarao et al., 2024) integrated part-of-speech information with pre-trained BERT models. The authors also showcased alternative approaches, including a rule-based system, LLMs, and traditional machine-learning models. These machine learning models used a comprehensive feature set, combining Abstract Meaning Representation features to capture deep semantic structures, part-of-speech (POS) tags for syntactic information, and other linguistic features.

**StaGE FriGHt** (Säuberli and Bodenmann, 2024) combined sequence labeling with dependency parsing. They used a fine-tuned BERT model to predict the head token of each statement span and expands the span using dependency relations.

**CUET_Big_O** upload a final submission entitled "Fine Tuned BERT". Unfortunately, we did not receive any information from the participants on how their system worked.

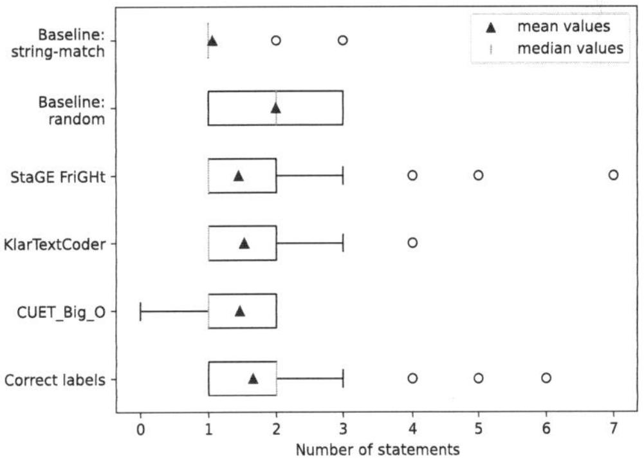


Figure 3: Distribution of the predicted number of statements.

### 5.3 Error Analysis

We further analyzed the submitted predictions. Figure 3 shows their distribution of the number of statements. The correct samples and the random baseline have the highest means, being the only systems with a median value of two. Especially the submission by CUET_Big_O overfits on the single statements samples, but also the other submissions have a bias toward the lower number of samples. Only the submission by StaGE FriGHt predicts more than four statements.

Furthermore, we analyzed in which cases the systems failed to predict the correct number of samples. For this, we compared the cases with our annotator agreement. Since two annotators reviewed the samples independently, we can identify challenging or non-trivial cases by their disagreement. For KlarTextCoder, 68.87% of the misclassified samples had a disagreement within the annotators. For the other two teams, these numbers were even higher, with 79.80% for StaGE FriGHt and 76.60% for CUET_Big_O. These numbers are higher than the overall annotator disagreement, indicating that the systems especially fail at the harder samples.

## 6 Discussion & Limitations

This shared task does not claim to solve the problem of statement segmentation conclusively. The main aim was to create the basis for practical applications and to ignite a scientific discussion. The most apparent limitation is the focus on mostly syntactic structures and often neglegting semantic relations and interpretation. This weakness becomes evident through a few examples.

Our statements focus mostly on chunks of information that need to be understood by the readers. Hence, we split sentences like "Eine Angel ist eine Schnur mit einem Haken." (*A fishing rod is a string with a hook.*) into two statements. From a content perspective, a fishing rod always consists of a string and a hook, so splitting these into two statements makes no sense. However, the reader still has to parse two separate statements independently: 1) there is a string, and 2) there is a hook. Therefore, we decided to split the sentence into two statements.

In contrast to this, we also discussed a few specifics, such as separated compound nouns, named entities, and dates, and combined them under the umbrella term "semantic units". For instance, "Berliner Fernsehturm ist ein Wahrzeichen der Stadt." (*Berlin's TV tower is a landmark of the city.*) in which only the combination of the two terms "Berlin's" and "TV tower" combined form the semantic unit behind the statement, i.e., one noun phrase.

Similarly, separated compound nouns, such as "Die Religion der Aleviten" (*Religion of the alevites.*) are not considered separate but as one named entity since it is synonymously with "Alevitentum" (*alevism*). Another case where semantics become very prominent is the case of idiomatic expressions and whether they should be treated as independent statements, as compound nouns, or as regular phrases. We made the practical decision to postpone this discussion, and we, therefore, annotated every sentence in which idioms occur as components with "0" (e.g., "Das A und O ist eine Redewendung" (*The alpha and omega is an idiom.*)).

Our shared task focuses on German Easy Language. While there are many similarities between Easy Language and standard German, our annotations cover the specifics of Easy Language. In Easy Language, writers are motivated to add explanations (section 5.2.2 in DIN-Normenausschuss Ergonomie 2023) to more complex terms. Therefore, there is an overamount of phrases like "das heißt" (*that means*) and "some say" (*manche sagen*). They most often function as an introductory phrase before the actual explanation, and thus, they don't convey information on their own. Hence, we ignored them in our statement annotations. Due to the focus on Easy Language specifics, the results cannot be directly transferred to standard German without further adaptions.

## 7 Conclusion

In the course of this shared task, we have presented both data and possible solutions to the problem of statement segmentation. Even if these results do not solve the problem conclusively, they nevertheless provide a valuable initial contribution to the discussion on the problem. We hope that future researchers will be able to draw further insights based on this foundation. The competition on codabench[11] is re-opened for further experiments and an easy comparison to the previous systems.

## Ethics statement

Since Easy Language has a vulnerable target group, special care should always be taken in this research field. As we do not create new texts in this task but merely conduct analyses on texts that have already been written, we do not see any direct risk of misuse or ethical implications. The results can

[11] https://www.codabench.org/competitions/3244/

be applied directly to German Easy Language, but we expect they could be generalized and used for simple languages from other nations as well.

## Acknowledgments

We are grateful to all the participants, whose enthusiastic participation made our shared task a great success.
This research has been partially funded by the German Federal Ministry of Education and Research (BMBF) through grant 01IS23069 Software Campus 3.0 (Technical University of Munich) as part of the Software Campus project "LIANA".
Thorben Schomacker received external funding from the IFB Hamburg as well as from the European Education and Culture Executive Agency.

## References

Fernando Alva-Manchego, Carolina Scarton, and Lucia Specia. 2020. Data-driven sentence simplification: Survey and benchmark. *Computational Linguistics*, 46(1):135–187.

Miriam Anschütz, Joshua Oehms, Thomas Wimmer, Bartłomiej Jezierski, and Georg Groh. 2023. Language models for German text simplification: Overcoming parallel data scarcity through style-specific pre-training. In *Findings of the Association for Computational Linguistics: ACL 2023*, pages 1147–1158, Toronto, Canada. Association for Computational Linguistics.

Ursula Bredel and Christiane Maaß. 2016. *Leichte Sprache theoretische Grundlagen, Orientierung für die Praxis*. Sprache im Blick. Dudenverlag.

Oscar M. Cumbicus-Pineda, Itziar Gonzalez-Dios, and Aitor Soroa. 2021. Linguistic Capabilities for a Checklist-based evaluation in Automatic Text Simplification. In *Proceedings of the First Workshop on Current Trends in Text Simplification (CTTS 2021)*, pages 70–83. CEUR-WS.

Silvana Deilen. 2020. Using eye-tracking to evaluate language processing in the easy language target group deilen/schiffl. *Easy language research: Text and user perspectives*, 2:273.

Silvana Deilen, Sergio Hernández Garrido, Ekaterina Lapshinova-Koltunski, and Christiane Maaß. 2023. Using ChatGPT as a CAT tool in easy language translation. In *Proceedings of the Second Workshop on Text Simplification, Accessibility and Readability*, pages 1–10, Varna, Bulgaria. INCOMA Ltd., Shoumen, Bulgaria.

DIN-Normenausschuss Ergonomie. 2023. Empfehlungen für Deutsche Leichte Sprache (DIN SPEC 33429).

Leon Fruth, Robin Jegan, and Andreas Henrich. 2024. An approach towards unsupervised text simplification on paragraph-level for German texts. In *Proceedings of the Workshop on DeTermIt! Evaluating Text Difficulty in a Multilingual Context @ LREC-COLING 2024*, pages 77–89, Torino, Italia. ELRA and ICCL.

Natalia Grabar and Horacio Saggion. 2022. Evaluation of automatic text simplification: Where are we now, where should we go from here. In *Actes de la 29e Conférence sur le Traitement Automatique des Langues Naturelles. Volume 1 : conférence principale*, pages 453–463, Avignon, France. ATALA.

Silvia Hansen-Schirra, Jean Nitzke, and Silke Gutermuth. 2021. *An Intralingual Parallel Corpus of Translations into German Easy Language (Geasy Corpus): What Sentence Alignments Can Tell Us About Translation Strategies in Intralingual Translation*, pages 281–298. Springer Singapore, Singapore.

Freya Hewett. 2023. APA-RST: A text simplification corpus with RST annotations. In *Proceedings of the 4th Workshop on Computational Approaches to Discourse (CODI 2023)*, pages 173–179, Toronto, Canada. Association for Computational Linguistics.

Sarah Jablotschkin, Elke Teich, and Heike Zinsmeister. 2024. DE-lite - a new corpus of easy German: Compilation, exploration, analysis. In *Proceedings of the Fourth Workshop on Language Technology for Equality, Diversity, Inclusion*, pages 106–117, St. Julian's, Malta. Association for Computational Linguistics.

Sarah Jablotschkin and Heike Zinsmeister. 2021. Annotating colon constructions in Easy and Plain German. In *Proceedings of the 3rd Swiss conference on barrier-free communication (BfC 2020)*, pages 125–134. ZHAW Zürcher Hochschule für Angewandte Wissenschaften.

Antoine Jamelot, Solen Quiniou, and Sophie Hamon. 2024. Improving text readability through segmentation into rheses. In *Proceedings of the 2024 Joint International Conference on Computational Linguistics, Language Resources and Evaluation (LREC-COLING 2024)*, pages 8925–8930, Torino, Italia. ELRA and ICCL.

Joongwon Kim, Mounica Maddela, Reno Kriz, Wei Xu, and Chris Callison-Burch. 2021. BiSECT: Learning to split and rephrase sentences with bitexts. In *Proceedings of the 2021 Conference on Empirical Methods in Natural Language Processing*, pages 6193–6209, Online and Punta Cana, Dominican Republic. Association for Computational Linguistics.

David Klaper, Sarah Ebling, and Martin Volk. 2013. Building a German/simple German parallel corpus for automatic text simplification. In *Proceedings of the Second Workshop on Predicting and Improving Text Readability for Target Reader Populations*, pages 11–19, Sofia, Bulgaria. Association for Computational Linguistics.

Ruben Klepp. 2022. Klassifizierung der Textkomplexität von Chatbot-Antworten mittels Transformer-Modellen. Master thesis, Hochschule Darmstadt, Germany.

Lars Klöser, Mika Beele, Jan-Niklas Schagen, and Bodo Kraft. 2024. German text simplification: Finetuning large language models with semi-synthetic data. In *Proceedings of the Fourth Workshop on Language Technology for Equality, Diversity, Inclusion*, pages 63–72, St. Julian's, Malta. Association for Computational Linguistics.

Chin-Yew Lin. 2004. ROUGE: A package for automatic evaluation of summaries. In *Text Summarization Branches Out*, pages 74–81, Barcelona, Spain. Association for Computational Linguistics.

Mounica Maddela, Yao Dou, David Heineman, and Wei Xu. 2023. LENS: A learnable evaluation metric for text simplification. In *Proceedings of the 61st Annual Meeting of the Association for Computational Linguistics (Volume 1: Long Papers)*, pages 16383–16408, Toronto, Canada. Association for Computational Linguistics.

Margot Madina, Itziar Gonzalez-Dios, and Melanie Siegel. 2023. Easy-to-read language resources and tools for three european languages. In *Proceedings of the 16th International Conference on PErvasive Technologies Related to Assistive Environments*, PETRA '23, page 693–699, New York, NY, USA. Association for Computing Machinery.

Margot Madina, Itziar Gonzalez-Dios, and Melanie Siegel. 2024. Towards Reliable E2R Texts: A Proposal for Standardized Evaluation Practices. In *Computers Helping People with Special Needs: 19th International Conference, ICCHP 2024, Linz, Austria, July 8–12, 2024, Proceedings, Part II*, pages 224–231, Berlin, Heidelberg. Springer-Verlag.

Sewon Min, Kalpesh Krishna, Xinxi Lyu, Mike Lewis, Wen-tau Yih, Pang Koh, Mohit Iyyer, Luke Zettlemoyer, and Hannaneh Hajishirzi. 2023. FActScore: Fine-grained atomic evaluation of factual precision in long form text generation. In *Proceedings of the 2023 Conference on Empirical Methods in Natural Language Processing*, pages 12076–12100, Singapore. Association for Computational Linguistics.

Salar Mohtaj, Babak Naderi, and Sebastian Möller. 2022. Overview of the GermEval 2022 shared task on text complexity assessment of German text. In *Proceedings of the GermEval 2022 Workshop on Text Complexity Assessment of German Text*, pages 1–9, Potsdam, Germany. Association for Computational Linguistics.

Netzwerk Leichte Sprache. 2022. Die Regeln für Leichte Sprache. `https://www.leichte-sprache.org/wp-content/uploads/2017/11/Regeln_Leichte_Sprache.pdf`. [Online; Last Update: *n/a*; Last Access: 2024-07-29].

Christina Niklaus, Matthias Cetto, André Freitas, and Siegfried Handschuh. 2019a. DisSim: A discourse-aware syntactic text simplification framework for English and German. In *Proceedings of the 12th International Conference on Natural Language Generation*, pages 504–507, Tokyo, Japan. Association for Computational Linguistics.

Christina Niklaus, André Freitas, and Siegfried Handschuh. 2019b. MinWikiSplit: A sentence splitting corpus with minimal propositions. In *Proceedings of the 12th International Conference on Natural Language Generation*, pages 118–123, Tokyo, Japan. Association for Computational Linguistics.

Kishore Papineni, Salim Roukos, Todd Ward, and Wei-Jing Zhu. 2002. Bleu: a method for automatic evaluation of machine translation. In *Proceedings of the 40th Annual Meeting of the Association for Computational Linguistics*, pages 311–318, Philadelphia, Pennsylvania, USA. Association for Computational Linguistics.

Maja Popović. 2015. chrF: character n-gram F-score for automatic MT evaluation. In *Proceedings of the Tenth Workshop on Statistical Machine Translation*, pages 392–395, Lisbon, Portugal. Association for Computational Linguistics.

Matt Post. 2018. A call for clarity in reporting BLEU scores. In *Proceedings of the Third Conference on Machine Translation: Research Papers*, pages 186–191, Brussels, Belgium. Association for Computational Linguistics.

Akhilesh Kakolu Ramarao, Wiebke Petersen, Anna Sophia Stein, Emma Stein, and Hanxin Xia. 2024. KlarTextCoders at StaGE: Automatic Statement Annotations for German Easy Language. In *Proceedings of the GermEval 2024 Shared Task on Statement Segmentation in German Easy Language (StaGE)*, Vienna, Austria. Association for Computational Linguistics.

Michael Ryan, Tarek Naous, and Wei Xu. 2023. Revisiting non-English text simplification: A unified multilingual benchmark. In *Proceedings of the 61st Annual Meeting of the Association for Computational Linguistics (Volume 1: Long Papers)*, pages 4898–4927, Toronto, Canada. Association for Computational Linguistics.

Andreas Säuberli and Niclas Bodenmann. 2024. Statement Segmentation for German Easy Language Using BERT and Dependency Parsing. In *Proceedings of the GermEval 2024 Shared Task on Statement Segmentation in German Easy Language (StaGE)*, Vienna, Austria. Association for Computational Linguistics.

Andreas Säuberli, Sarah Ebling, and Martin Volk. 2020. Benchmarking data-driven automatic text simplification for German. In *Proceedings of the 1st Workshop on Tools and Resources to Empower People with*

*REAding DIfficulties (READI)*, pages 41–48, Marseille, France. European Language Resources Association.

Andreas Säuberli, Franz Holzknecht, Patrick Haller, Silvana Deilen, Laura Schiffl, Silvia Hansen-Schirra, and Sarah Ebling. 2024. Digital Comprehensibility Assessment of Simplified Texts among Persons with Intellectual Disabilities. In *Proceedings of the CHI Conference on Human Factors in Computing Systems*, CHI '24, New York, NY, USA. Association for Computing Machinery.

Thorben Schomacker, Michael Gille, Marina Tropmann-Frick, and Jörg von der Hülls. 2023. Data and approaches for German text simplification – towards an accessibility-enhanced communication. In *Proceedings of the 19th Conference on Natural Language Processing (KONVENS 2023)*, pages 63–68, Ingolstadt, Germany. Association for Computational Linguistics.

Thorben Schomacker, Michael Gille, Marina Tropmann-Frick, and Jörg von der Hülls. 2024. Self-regulated and Participatory Automatic Text Simplification. In *Applied Machine Learning and Data Analytics*, Communications in Computer and Information Science, pages 264–273, Cham. Springer Nature Switzerland.

Matthew Shardlow, Fernando Alva-Manchego, Riza Batista-Navarro, Stefan Bott, Saul Calderon Ramirez, Rémi Cardon, Thomas François, Akio Hayakawa, Andrea Horbach, Anna Hülsing, Yusuke Ide, Joseph Marvin Imperial, Adam Nohejl, Kai North, Laura Occhipinti, Nelson Peréz Rojas, Nishat Raihan, Tharindu Ranasinghe, Martin Solis Salazar, Sanja Štajner, Marcos Zampieri, and Horacio Saggion. 2024. The BEA 2024 shared task on the multilingual lexical simplification pipeline. In *Proceedings of the 19th Workshop on Innovative Use of NLP for Building Educational Applications (BEA 2024)*, pages 571–589, Mexico City, Mexico. Association for Computational Linguistics.

Advaith Siddharthan. 2014. A survey of research on text simplification. *ITL - International Journal of Applied Linguistics*, 165(2):259–298. Publisher: John Benjamins.

Melanie Siegel, Dorothee Beermann, and Lars Hellan. 2019. Aspects of Linguistic Complexity: A German – Norwegian Approach to the Creation of Resources for Easy-To-Understand Language. In *2019 Eleventh International Conference on Quality of Multimedia Experience (QoMEX)*, pages 1–3. IEEE.

Nicolas Spring, Annette Rios, and Sarah Ebling. 2021. Exploring German multi-level text simplification. In *Proceedings of the International Conference on Recent Advances in Natural Language Processing (RANLP 2021)*, pages 1339–1349, Held Online. INCOMA Ltd.

Sanja Stajner. 2021. Automatic text simplification for social good: Progress and challenges. In *Findings of the Association for Computational Linguistics: ACL-IJCNLP 2021*, pages 2637–2652, Online. Association for Computational Linguistics.

Sanja Štajner, Horacio Saggio, Matthew Shardlow, and Fernando Alva-Manchego, editors. 2023. *Proceedings of the Second Workshop on Text Simplification, Accessibility and Readability*. INCOMA Ltd., Shoumen, Bulgaria, Varna, Bulgaria.

Regina Stodden. 2024. Reproduction of German text simplification systems. In *Proceedings of the Workshop on DeTermIt! Evaluating Text Difficulty in a Multilingual Context @ LREC-COLING 2024*, pages 1–15, Torino, Italia. ELRA and ICCL.

Regina Stodden, Omar Momen, and Laura Kallmeyer. 2023. DEplain: A German parallel corpus with intralingual translations into plain language for sentence and document simplification. In *Proceedings of the 61st Annual Meeting of the Association for Computational Linguistics (Volume 1: Long Papers)*, pages 16441–16463, Toronto, Canada. Association for Computational Linguistics.

Elior Sulem, Omri Abend, and Ari Rappoport. 2018. Semantic structural evaluation for text simplification. In *Proceedings of the 2018 Conference of the North American Chapter of the Association for Computational Linguistics: Human Language Technologies, Volume 1 (Long Papers)*, pages 685–696, New Orleans, Louisiana. Association for Computational Linguistics.

Julia Suter, Sarah Ebling, and Martin Volk. 2016. Rule-based Automatic Text Simplification for German. In *Proceedings of the 13th Conference on Natural Language Processing*, pages 279–287.

Vanessa Toborek, Moritz Busch, Malte Boßert, Christian Bauckhage, and Pascal Welke. 2023. A new aligned simple German corpus. In *Proceedings of the 61st Annual Meeting of the Association for Computational Linguistics (Volume 1: Long Papers)*, pages 11393–11412, Toronto, Canada. Association for Computational Linguistics.

Jan Trienes, Jörg Schlötterer, Hans-Ulrich Schildhaus, and Christin Seifert. 2022. Patient-friendly clinical notes: Towards a new text simplification dataset. In *Proceedings of the Workshop on Text Simplification, Accessibility, and Readability (TSAR-2022)*, pages 19–27, Abu Dhabi, United Arab Emirates (Virtual). Association for Computational Linguistics.

Seid Muhie Yimam, Chris Biemann, Shervin Malmasi, Gustavo Paetzold, Lucia Specia, Sanja Štajner, Anaïs Tack, and Marcos Zampieri. 2018. A report on the complex word identification shared task 2018. In *Proceedings of the Thirteenth Workshop on Innovative Use of NLP for Building Educational Applications*, pages 66–78, New Orleans, Louisiana. Association for Computational Linguistics.

| Team | Task 1 | | | | | Task 2 | |
|---|---|---|---|---|---|---|---|
| | MAE↓ | MSE↓ | Prec↑ | Rec↑ | F1↑ | chrF↑ | jaccard↑ |
| KlarTextCoder | **0.35** | **0.41** | **0.65** | **0.68** | **0.66** | **0.36** | 0.29 |
| StaGE FriGHt | 0.40 | 0.55 | **0.65** | 0.66 | 0.64 | 0.30 | **0.38** |
| CUET_Big_O | 0.40 | 0.5 | 0.57 | 0.64 | 0.61 | - | - |
| Baseline: string-match | 0.60 | 0.91 | 0.53 | 0.53 | 0.41 | 0.05 | 0.04 |
| Baseline: random | 0.92 | 1.41 | 0.38 | 0.31 | 0.33 | 0.24 | 0.27 |
| Baseline: all-1 | 0.66 | 1.05 | 0.25 | 0.50 | 0.33 | 0.00 | 0.00 |

Table 4: Detailed results. The F1-scores averages are weighted by the support of the respective class

## A Annotation guidelines v0.1

Our data samples are single sentences. We split sentences at punctuation marks. Hence, they can span over several lines. We annotate the sentences by the number of statements contained in them. The tokens in the sentence are separated by whitespaces. A statement only contains full tokens; we don't split tokens for subtoken annotations. If a sentence spans several lines (as typical for Leichte Sprache), the line breaks are displayed with "\newline". Newlines could help classification models in the future, and thus, they are given as separate tokens but should be ignored during annotation.

We do not correct any typos or parsing errors. Thus, the samples can contain punctuation or grammatical errors. If the errors are severe, e.g., if two sentences are merged into one due to missing punctuations, these samples are annotated as erroneous. The annotations process is split into two parts, similar to our subtasks. First, we determined the number of statements and then annotated the statement spans.

### A.1 Determining the number of statements / Statement separation

Ideally, a statement is formed by a Subject-Verb-Object (SVO) combination or additional adjectives or prepositional constructions that could form a separate sentence. Example: "Die moderne Sportart heißt: \newline Splashdiving." (*The modern sport is called: \newline Splashdiving*) contains 2 statements, one for the main SVO combination "Die Sportart heißt Splashdiving", and one for the additional adjection "moderne". The sentences don't have to be in proper SVC order, as subclauses can form a statement without any main clause. As a rule of thumb, one statement contains only one full verb at maximum (yet auxiliary and full verbs can be together).

A sentence is split into multiple sentences based on the criteria discussed in the following subsections.

#### A.1.1 Separating via conjunctions

Conjunctions are used to connect clauses within a sentence. There are two types of conjunctions: Coordinating and subordinating conjunctions. Coordinating conjunctions connect two main clauses. Subordinating conjunctions, in contrast, connect a main clause with a subordinate clause, emphasizing the main clause more than the subordinate clause. Both clauses form separate statements in our annotations.

**Special case: "Manche sagen" (*Some say*) and "Das heißt" (*That means*)** "Das heißt, .." is a common construction in Leichte Sprache. These phrases are not counted as separate statements. However, if the phrase contains additional information, such as "Lügen heißt.." (*Lying means*) or "Manche Politiker sagen.." (*Some politicians say*), these phrases are annotated as usual. Only the very specific formulations above are an exception.

**Special case: Parentheses** Information in parentheses is always a separate statement.

#### A.1.2 Separating via single adjectives/adverbials

Nouns are often further described by adjectives. If these adjectives give additional information or restrict the noun to a subgroup, these adjectives form a separate statement. In the first example in Table 5, the adjective modern gives additional information about the sport, so it is extracted as a new statement. In contrast, if the adjective/adverb gives no further restrictions, it is not counted as a separate statement. If multiple adjectives/adverbs are concatenated into a sequence, each of them forms a single statement (see Table 5).

| Sentence | Translation | # stmts | Explanation |
|---|---|---|---|
| Die moderne Sportart heißt: \newline Splashdiving. | The modern sport is called: \newline Splashdiving. | 2 | "modern" gives additional information about the sport |
| Der Vorschlag wurde ohne Gegenstimmen angenommen. | The proposal was accepted without any opposing votes. | 2 | Modal adverbial "ohne Gegenstimmen" |
| Die Einwohner konnten ihre Lebensmittel ganz normal kaufen. | The inhabitants were able to buy their food as normal. | 1 | "ganz normal" gives no restrictions |
| Die Mitarbeiter reparieren gemeinsam kaputte Dinge. | The employees repair broken things together. | 2 | Sequence: The employees repair broken things. The employees repair things together. |

Table 5: Example sentences and explanations for their annotated number of statements.

**Special case: Quantifiers** Quantifiers like "viele" (*many*), "alle" (*all*), "mache" (*some*) or counts like "50 Menschen" (*50 people*) are no separate statements.

**Special case: Filler words** Filler words like "sehr" (*very*), "oft" (*often*), "darum" (*therefore*), or "auch" (*also*) are no separate statements.

**Special case: Comparatives and superlatives** Comparatives and superlatives in constructions like "größte Stadt" (*biggest city*) or "weniger Menschen" (*fewer people*) are closely connected to their noun and, thus, form no separate statement.

### A.1.3 Separating via prepositional phrase

Prepositional often specify things and actions, e.g., by indicating ownership ("von .." (*by*)), a direction ("nach .." (*to*)), or modality ("mit .." (*with*)). Similar to adjectives, this additional information forms a new statement. For example, the sentence "Man kann mit einem Fahr-stuhl nach oben fahren." (*You can go to the top in an elevator.*) contains the prepositional phrases "mit einem Fahrstuhl" and "ach oben", thus containing two statements. If multiple prepositional phrases are stacked after another, each of them forms a separate statement.

**Special case: Composites** The German language gives the option to stack multiple pieces of information into one word (so-called composite words). Prepositional phrases that can be rephrased to a single word (e.g., "Religion der Christen" (*religion of the Christians*) $\rightarrow$ "Christentum" (*Christianity*); "Mitglied in der Partei" (*member of the party*) $\rightarrow$ "Parteimitglied" (*party member*)) are no additional statement.

**Speical case: Trivial prepositions** Sometimes, the verb already contains the information in the prepositional phrase (e.g., "in die Luft sprengen" (*lit: blow up into the air*)). Then, we don't annotate the prepositional phrases as separate statements.

**Special case: Date and year specifications** Dates are annotated as separate statements except if the remaining statement only states that something exists or was born. For example, in the sentence "Im Jahr 1877 heiraten Alexander Graham Bell und Mabel Hubbard." (*In 1877, Alexander Graham Bell and Mabel Hubbard marry.*), the year and the marriage itself are two different statements. However, in the sentence "Angela Merkel wurde am 17. Juli 1954 geboren." (*Angela Merkel was born on July 17, 1954.,*), the information that she was born is trivial. Thus, the sentence contains only 1 statement. In contrast, abstract time information like "manchmal"sometimes or "immer" (*always*) is no separate statement.

### A.1.4 4. 0-statement sentences or un-parseable sentences (= erroneous samples)

There can be samples that don't contain a statement, e.g., if there are problems with the preprocessing and there are multiple sentences in the sample. Also, sentences that don't contain a verb, like "An der Universität Boston." (*At the university of Boston.*), are annotated with 0.

| Sentence | Translation | # stmts | Spans | Explanation |
|---|---|---|---|---|
| 0:=Die 1:=moderne 2:=Sportart 3:=heißt: 4:= 5:=\newline 6:=Splashdiving. | 0:=The 1:=modern 2:=sport 3:=is called: 5:=\newline 6:=Splashdiving. | 2 | [[1], [3,6]] | Tokens 0, 4, 5 are never annotated. Token 2 (Sportart) is in both spans, so it is not stated explicitly. |
| 0:=Der 1:=Vorschlag 2:=wurde 3:=ohne 4:=Gegenstimmen 5:=angenommen. | 0:=The 1:=proposal 2:=was 5:=accepted 3:=without 4:=opposing votes. | 2 | [[1,2,5], [3,4]] | No overlaps between statements |
| 0:=Die 1:=Einwohner 2:=konnten 3:=ihre 4:=Lebensmittel 5:=ganz 6:=normal 7:=kaufen. | 0:=The 1:=inhabitants 2:=could 7:=buy 3:=their 4:=food 5:=as 6:=normal. | 1 | | No spans for sentences with one statement |
| 0:=Die 1:=Mitarbeiter 2:=reparieren 3:=gemeinsam 4:=kaputte 5:=Dinge. | 0:=The 1:=employees 2:=repair 4:=broken 5:=things 3:=together. | 2 | [[3], [4,5]] | We identified two statements in this sentence ("0:=Die 1:=Mitarbeiter 2:=reparieren 3:=gemeinsam." and "0:=Die 1:=Mitarbeiter 2:=reparieren 4:=kaputte 5:=Dinge."). The tokens 2 and 3 ("Mitarbeiter reparieren") are contained in both statements, so we don't include them in the annotations. The tokens 3 ("gemeinsam") and 4,5 ("kaputte Dinge") are independant, and hence, form the two statement spans. |

Table 6: Example sentences and their statement span annotations. The indexes of the English translations are use the same as the German original. Hence, they are not in ascending order and more than one English word may be related to one German word.

# KlarTextCoders at StaGE:
# Automatic Statement Annotations for *German Easy Language*

**Akhilesh Kakolu Ramarao[1], Wiebke Petersen[1], Anna Sophia Stein[1], Emma Stein[2], Hanxin Xia[1]**
Heinrich-Heine-Universität[1], Georg-August-Universität[2]
{akhilesh.kakolu.ramarao,wiebke.petersen,anna.stein,hanxin.xia}@uni-duesseldorf.de,
emma.stein@stud.uni-goettingen.de

## Abstract

This paper presents our approach to the GermEval 2024 task, "Statement Segmentation in German Easy Language (StaGE)," addressing both subtasks: predicting the number of statements and identifying statement spans. We introduce a novel method integrating part-of-speech information with pre-trained BERT models, achieving leading performance in both the subtasks. For the statement count prediction (subtask 1), our model achieved a precision of 0.65, a recall of 0.68, and an F1-score of 0.65, with a Mean Absolute Error (MAE) of 0.36 and Mean Squared Error (MSE) of 0.43. For statement span annotation (subtask 2), we adapted our BERT model (used for subtask 1) to perform token-level classification, achieving a chrF score of 0.36 and a Jaccard similarity of 0.29. We also detail our exploration of alternative approaches to the shared task, including a rule-based system, LLMs, and traditional machine learning models. These machine learning models used a comprehensive feature set, combining Abstract Meaning Representation (AMR) features to capture deep semantic structures, part-of-speech (POS) tags for syntactic information, and other linguistic features.

**Keywords:** Automatic Text Simplification, Leichte Sprache, Statement Segmentation, German Easy Language.

## 1 Introduction

Easy Language is a simplified linguistic form that excludes complex grammatical and lexical features (Maaß and Bredel, 2017). Using German Easy Language, or: *Leichte Sprache* named in original German concepts, offers substantial advantages to a diverse range of users. A recent LEO study found that 6.2 million Germans have a low literacy level and struggle with reading simple sentences (Buddeberg and Grotlüschen, 2020). This includes, for example, individuals who are not native speakers of German or those with learning disabilities. However, other groups may also benefit from Easy Language: educators and therapists may find these adaptations beneficial in making educational materials more accessible and engaging. Furthermore, governmental entities sharing complex legal or bureaucratic information can leverage these tools to ensure their communications are comprehensible to a broader audience, potentially enhancing civic participation and adherence to regulations. Since 2011, German regulatory frameworks have mandated that governance bodies ensure their online content conforms to higher accessibility standards (Bundesministerium des Innern und für Heimat, 2011). This includes mandatory German Easy Language information on the main contents of the website, notes on navigating the website, and further information available in German Sign Language and in Easy Language.

Developing an algorithm capable of annotating statements in Easy Language could significantly streamline the process of composing and reviewing such texts, simplifying the publication of German Easy Language materials. Additionally, this technology could increase the quality of these texts by providing authors with deeper insights into the prevalence of specific statements within a text.

To foster this development, the "Statement Segmentation in German Easy Language (StaGE)" workshop from this year's GermEval task is comprised of two sub-tasks. The first task (subtask 1) involves predicting the number of statements for the given dataset, while the second task (subtask 2) asks to predict the position of the statement spans. The data for this task consists of Easy Language sentences sampled from Hurraki[1], an encyclopedia similar to Wikipedia for German Easy Language. For subtask 1, our submitted model achieved a 0.35 mean accuracy error (precision: 0.66, recall: 0.68,

[1]https://hurraki.de/wiki/Hauptseite

f1-score: 0.66) on the provided evaluation set. For the subtask 2, our submitted model achieved a chrF score of 0.36 and a Jaccard similarity of 0.29.

Our main contributions are: 1) We presented a multi-faceted approach to the shared task, using rule-based parser, machine learning classifiers with various linguistic features, Large Language Models (LLMs) and fine-tuning pretrained language model. 2) Integration of part-of-speech (POS) information with pre-trained language model for both subtasks. 3) We approached the statement span annotation task (subtask 2) as a token-level classification problem. This allowed the model to leverage transfer learning from the broader statement-level classification task (subtask 1).

All the code and data are available on GitHub[2].

## 2 Background

Text simplification has been an ongoing task attracting joint efforts from researchers of various disciplines across the globe (Shardlow, 2014). Although initially conceptualized as a method reducing the processing load of NLP systems by reducing text complexity (Chandrasekar and Srinivas, 1997), the application areas of Easy Language have expanded to assisting individuals with low literacy and reading comprehension difficulties, enhancing L2 language acquisition and facilitating the integration of migrants (Al-Thanyyan and Azmi, 2021; Steinmetz and Harbusch, 2022; Bock, 2014).

In the German context, governmental mandates aimed at improving public accessibility have led to the widespread availability of German Easy Language texts, known as *Leichte Sprache*, on the Internet (Ebling et al., 2022; Asghari et al., 2023). This has also led to the creation of text-based corpora such as, the document-level aligned corpus created by Gonzales et al. (2021), which contains full articles paired with simplified summaries collected from Swiss news magazine *20 Minuten*, and sentence-level aligned Simple German dataset curated by Toborek et al. (2023).

Early approaches to automatic text simplification in German focused on rule-based methods, such as the system developed by Suter et al. (2016), which primarily used syntactic transformation rules. Subsequent studies introduced discourse-based techniques (Niklaus et al., 2019) and lexical simplification strategies (Siegel et al., 2019).

More recent research viewed text simplification as a sequence-to-sequence task, where the input is a complex text and the output is a simplified version of the same text. For instance, Säuberli et al. (2020); Spring et al. (2021); Ebling et al. (2022) used transformer-based (Vaswani et al., 2017) sequence-to-sequence models. Gonzales et al. (2021) further extended this approach by fine-tuning mBART (Liu et al., 2020) model. Additionally, prompting techniques have been explored by Ryan et al. (2023) and Alva-Manchego et al. (2021), while Mallinson et al. (2020) used few-shot and zero-shot learning using BLOOM model (Scao et al., 2023). A thorough evaluation of the neural approaches is presented in Stodden (2024), providing a comprehensive comparison of their performance.

Despite these advancements, the automatic text simplification for German texts remains a persitent challenge (Schomacker et al., 2023). A major challenge in automatic text simplification is accurately identifying individual statements within complex sentences, a crucial step in improving the effectiveness of current simplification methods.

## 3 Task

The following section briefly outlines the "Statement Segmentation in German Easy Language (StaGE)" task at GermEval 2024 (Schomacker et al., 2024).

### 3.1 Annotation guidelines

A sentence in German Easy Language differs from regular language in a couple of ways and should adhere to its own set of rules. Ideally, a sentence in *Leichte Sprache* contains three arguments: subject, object, and verb. Additional information will be regarded as extra statements. The provided annotation guidelines[3] follow the recommendations drafted in the DIN SPEC 33429[4].

### 3.2 Dataset

For the task, four datasets are provided by the organizers, three reserved for development (train, trial, and test) and one for evaluation (eval). The trial set is the smallest split with 26 sentences, followed by test with 416, and finally, training with 1,530 sentences. The number-of-statement counts for each

[2]https://github.com/ansost/easy-to-read

[3]https://german-easy-to-read.github.io/statements/annotations/

[4]https://www.dinmedia.de/de/technische-regel-entwurf/din-spec-33429/364785446. Last accessed: 2nd August, 2024.

split can be seen in Table 1.

The small trial set was available at the start of the task for a general overview. Train data was then published for initial model development. Then the test set was released to enhance the development. Finally, eval was made public for blind model evaluation and scoring.

The train set has a token count of 5,093 with an average sentence length of 7.59. The token count and average sentence length of the test set are 1,142 and 7.35. Sentences in the eval set contain 7.54 tokens on average.

| n. statements | trial | train | test | eval |
|---|---|---|---|---|
| 0 | 1 | 449 | - | - |
| 1 | 15 | 1530 | 258 | 437 |
| 2 | 9 | 732 | 123 | 332 |
| 3 | 1 | 191 | 28 | 89 |
| 4 | - | 38 | 6 | 14 |
| 5 | - | 3 | 1 | 5 |
| 6 | - | 1 | - | 1 |

Table 1: Distribution of number of statements in trial, test and train.

## 4 Methodology

In this section, we describe different methods used in our study. We begin by explaining the Rule-based parser (Section 4.1), features used for machine learning classifiers (Section 4.2), BERT (Section 4.3) and finally the Large Language Models (LLMs) (Section 4.4).

### 4.1 Rule-based

We built a rule-based parser based on the annotation guidelines provided by the organizers. We used the German language model from SpaCy's *de_dep_news_trf*[5], which was trained on a dataset of German news articles. We began by performing a token-level analysis, where we iterated over each token in the sentence. For each token, we extracted the part-of-speech tag, dependency label, and morphological features using the parser mentioned above. Tokens in parentheses were counted as separate statements. Adjectives with noun heads were also counted, and they functioned as separate statements. Conversely, quantifiers, filler words, comparatives, and superlatives did not constitute independent statements.

In the next step, we checked for the existence of propositional phrases and their positioning in a sentence to see whether they added a new statement or not. For example, if a propositional phrase was part of a larger composite phrase, we counted it as one statement instead of multiple separate statements. Similarly, trivial propositions were not counted as separate statements. A sentence with date and year was treated as a distinct statement.

We then grouped tokens into clauses based on their dependencies and part-of-speech tags. We analyzed each clause to determine if it contained a subject, verb, or object. The clauses that met this criteria were treated as separate statements.

### 4.2 Feature-based

In order to experiment with classical feature-based machine learning approaches, a set of features has been extracted.

#### 4.2.1 Feature extraction

The features were chosen to cover a spectrum of linguistic characteristics as broad and diverse as possible. This includes features extracted from syntax trees, features of meaning representations, simple length features and embedding vectors contextualized by a LLM. Some features have been inspired by our previous work on judging text simplicity (Arps et al., 2022) and on machine generated text detection (Ciccarelli et al., 2024). Altogether, we extracted 3,968 features, of which we kept only those 1,310. which applied to at least five items from the union of the train and the trial data.

**Dependency tree features** We parsed the phrases using the dependency tree parser with Spacy's *de_core_news_sm*[6] language model (the small model was used due to computational limitations). For each dependency tree, we have extracted all maximal paths, starting from the root node. From these, we extracted as features: 1) all dependency sequences of the maximal paths and their prefixes and 2) all pairings of maximal dependency paths with the POS tag of their nodes. Figure 1 (appendix) illustrates the extracted features. Furthermore, we included some more general features like minimal/maximal/average length of dependency chains, number of roots and number of root childs. All this resulted in 2,146 dependency tree features (of which 388 were kept as they apply to at least five items in train and trial).

[5]https://spacy.io/models/de

[6]https://spacy.io/models/de

**AMR features** To capture semantic features as well, we decided to use abstract meaning representations (AMRs) as a further source of features. AMR is a semantic representation framework that abstracts the meaning of a text by focusing on predicate-argument structure rather than surface form. It was first introduced in Langkilde and Knight (1998), and due to strict format specifications, it became one of the most influential representation formats for semantic parsing (Banarescu et al., 2013). Due to availability and performance, we have opted for the *amrlib* library for English.[7] Therefore we translated all texts to English using *GoogleTranslator* from the *deep-translator* library[8]. The translated texts were then parsed into AMRs. Similar to the dependency trees, we traversed the AMR, starting from the root node and collecting attribute paths as features. The main difference is that AMRs are not trees but general acyclic graphs. The following features have been collected (see Figure 2 in Appendix A for illustration): a) all attribute sequences starting at the root; b) each maximal path additionally paired with the instance types of its leave. Altogether this resulted in 1,776 AMR-features (888 apply to at least five items in train and trial).

**Additional linguistic features** Furthermore, we collected additional linguistic features. These features include simple counting features like number of tokens, mean number of characters per word, or number of punctuation counts and counts of important part-of-speech tags obtained via Spacy verb|de_dep_news_trf|; Spacy ver. 3.7.5;[9] Honnibal and Montani (2020).

For further syntactic features, we used the Berkeley Neural Parser (Kitaev et al., 2019; Kitaev and Klein, 2018)[10]. The direct results returned by the parser are NLTK tree forms (see Figure 3).

Based on the tree form of each sentence we extracted multiple features based on pre-defined rules for training the classifiers: 1) For NPs that contain more than two words (not only article and noun root), we count each occurrence within the sentence, so if a sentence has five such NPs, we record the big NP count as 5; 2) For Prepositional Phrases (PPs) that contain more than three words, we count each occurrence within the sentence, so if a sentence has two such PPs, we record the big PP count as 2; 3) If neither "(S" nor "(V" is present in the tree form, the current instance is not a sentence, i.e., 0-statement;.

Additionally, two readability formulas defined in the *textstat* library, namely Flesch and of the Wiener Sachtextformel (variant 1), have been applied to the phrases[11]. These formulas try to estimate how easy a text is to read on the basis of words per sentence and syllable or character per word counts. Both measures are specially designed to estimate the readability of German texts.

We also used a language complexity classification pipeline, which classifies texts into four language complexity classes and assigns them a score. Only the score was used as a feature [12].

Finally, the predictions on the number of statements made by the rule-based account as described in Section 4.1 has been added as an additional feature as well. Altogether, this group of additional features consists of 32 features (25 are kept, as they apply to at least five items in train and trial).

**BERT features** The BERT model *bert-base-german-cased* has been used without any finetuning to extract the last hidden state of the CLS token that can be seen as an embedding of the phrase.[13] Uniform Manifold Approximation and Projection (UMAP) has been used to reduce the number of dimensions to 10. The resulting 10 dimensions were used as additional features.

#### 4.2.2 Data augmentation

In order to account for the unbalanced training set, in which more than 60% of the data belongs to the class '1 statement', we have decided to augment the data by round-trip translation. Therefore, all items with more than one statement have been translated into Finnish and back using Google Translator, and all examples with more than two statements have additionally been translated into Mandarin and back. Finnish and Mandarin were selected to maximize contrast with German. Neither language belongs to the Indo-European language family, and they represent opposite ends of the morphological spectrum. While Chinese is an isolating language, Finnish is agglutinative, providing a stark contrast to the inflectional nature of German.

[7] https://github.com/bjascob/amrlib
[8] https://pypi.org/project/deep-translator/
[9] https://spacy.io/models/de#de_dep_news_trf
[10] https://github.com/nikitakit/self-attentive-parser
[11] https://pypi.org/project/textstat/
[12] https://huggingface.co/krupper/text-complexity-classification
[13] https://huggingface.co/dbmdz/bert-base-german-cased

The idea is that this contrast in language structure reveals the underlying semantic content through roundtrip translations. It turned out that cases in which the re-translation matched the original were rare enough (for Finnish 6.6%, for Mandarin 3%) to be ignored. Thus, by the round-trip translation method new trainings data with differing feature values could be gained. We assumed that the number of statements is not affected by the translations.

### 4.3 BERT

We use BERT (Bidirectional Encoder Representations from Transformers) (Devlin et al., 2019) specifically *bert-base-german-cased*[14]. We further adapted this model by fine-tuning it for the subtasks, explained in Sections 5.1 and 5.2.

### 4.4 LLMs

Since Large Language Models are already finding various applications in the area of text simplification Tan et al. (2024); Baez and Saggion (2023), we wanted to explore how LLMs perform for annotating statements in simplified language.

We used *LLaMA-3-70B-Instruct* [15] for our analysis. To design the prompt, we started out with a simple one-shot prompt: "How many statements does this sentence have?". This prompt was then iteratively improved. One of the first changes we made was adding few-shot prompting and providing the model with example annotations from the training data in the prompt.

We also tested multiple ways of providing the annotation guidelines and specific rules from those annotation guidelines to the model. Automatic chain of thought prompting was also added since it has been shown to improve LLM performance in the past (Wei et al., 2022; Zhang et al., 2022). Initially, the prompts were given over *Huggingchat*[16], but an API provided faster and more reproducible results. This way, it allowed us to provide one sentence at a time instead of chunks of the dataset, which also improved performance. We also incorporated both system and user-level prompts and instructed the LLM to return the data in a specific format for easier analysis of the results. We used *LLaMA* model through an API endpoint provided by the KISSKI AI Service Centre for Sensitive and Critical Infrastructures[17]. All queries were made using a seed to ensure reproducibility. Models, scripts, prompts, and hyperparameters can be found on our GitHub.

[14] `https://huggingface.co/google-bert/bert-base-german-cased`

[15] `https://huggingface.co/meta-LLaMA/Meta-LLaMA-3-70B-Instruct`

[16] `https://huggingface.co/chat/`

## 5 Experiments

In this section, we provide a detailed evaluation of our approach to the shared task, specifying how we built the rule-based parser, different machine learning classifiers, and used Large Language Models (LLMs) (mentioned in Section 4).

### 5.1 Subtask 1: Determining the number of statements

The performance results of our models tackling subtask 1, as described in Section 4, are stated in Table 2 and compared to a most frequent class dummy classifier (MFC, model 0).

| Nr | Model | Data | MAE | Acc |
|---|---|---|---|---|
| **Most frequent class dummy classifier** | | | | |
| 0 | MFC | ttt | 0.655 | 0.499 |
| **Rule-based parser** | | | | |
| 1 | RuleParser | tt | 0.891 | 0.336 |
| **Feature-based (baselines)** | | | | |
| 2 | MLP+allFeat | ttt | 0.426 | 0.622 |
| 3 | SVM+allFeat | ttt | 0.449 | 0.618 |
| 4 | LR+allFeat | ttt | 0.376 | 0.663 |
| 5 | RF+allFeat | ttt | 0.377 | 0.67 |
| **Feature-based (feature subsets + augmented data)** | | | | |
| 6 | LR+allFeat | ttt+au | 0.367 | 0.67 |
| 7 | RF+allFeat | ttt+au | 0.354 | 0.688 |
| 8 | RF+BERTFeat | ttt | 0.625 | 0.498 |
| 9 | RF+AMRFeat | ttt | 0.559 | 0.544 |
| 10 | RF+DepTreeFeat | ttt | 0.419 | 0.634 |
| 11 | RF+addFeat | ttt | 0.39 | 0.646 |
| 12 | LR-75-per-type | ttt+au | 0.331 | 0.698 |
| 13 | LR-200-overall | ttt+au | 0.328 | 0.698 |
| **LLMs** | | | | |
| 14* | LLMPrompting | tt | – – | 0.668 |
| **15** | **BERT+POStags** | **90%ttt** | **0.36** | **0.689** |

Table 2: Performance comparison of different models tested on the eval data for subtask 1 (models marked by $*$ are trained and tested only on the original data sets). Training data differs (ttt: original train, trial and test data, ttt+au: ttt plus augmented data as described in Section 4.2.2). The feature-based approaches have been trained on all (allFeat) or a subset of the features as described in Section 4.2.

**Rule-based parser** Our initial approach to the task involved developing a rule-based parser that followed the annotation guidelines provided by the organizers (refer Section 4.1). The parser was then trained on the provided training dataset of 2,989 samples. It achieved an accuracy of 57% on the test dataset (consisting of 417 samples).

[17] `https://kisski.gwdg.de/`

**Feature-based classifiers** We tested four different machine learning classifiers implemented in Scikit-Learn (Pedregosa et al., 2011): Random Forest (RF), Support-Vector-Machine (SVM), Multilayer-Perceptron (MLP) and a logistic regression (LR) model (see Table 2, model 2-5). All classifier parameters have been set to the default values (for the MLP one hidden layer of size 128 was chosen).

Each classifier was trained on the combined train, trial and test set and evaluated against the eval set. Zero-statements were removed from all splits. In the training all features described in Section 4.2 have been used if they were attested for at least 5 phrases in the train and trial set. Table 2 shows that all classifiers beat the dummy baseline (MFC) and that RF and LR perform best of the baselines by outperforming MFC by 0.17 for accuracy (Acc.) and 0.28 for mean absolute error (MAE).

As on the original train and test data provided by the organizers, RF slightly outperformed LR all further experiments have been done with RF. Augmentating the training data did improve the results only slightly (compare model 7 to 5 and model 6 to 4 in Table 2). Additionally, we tested how different subsets of the feature set influence the performance (models 8-11 in Table 2). The additional linguistic features ('Add.') performed best, followed closely by the dependency tree features (DepTreeFeat). Significantly worse are the AMR and the BERT features (in this order).

To get a better grip on our features we have extracted from a Random Forest classifier the importance rankings for the features. Tables 3, 4 and 5 in Appendix show the 10 most important features for the first three classes. The 20 most important features over all classes can be seen in Table 6. It turns out that length features (length of the AMR representation, length of the maximal dependency chain, number of tokens, ...) are the most important features for classification. That was to be expected as longer sentences tend to include more statements. Interestingly, although a classifier trained solely on the BERT features (Table 2, model 7) does not perform very well, all 10 BERT features (UMAP0 up to UMAP9) belong to the overall top 20 features (see Table 6).

Based on the feature importance scores we trained LR models on feature subsets. As data augmentation lead at least to a slight improvement, we included the augmented data into our training data. First, we selected for each feature type class the n most important features (if available). We tested for n between 5 and 150 of which n=75 turned out best (see model 12 in Table 2). Second, we considered all features at once and selected the n overall most important features testing for n between 5 and 1,000. Here, n=200 turned out best (see model 13 in Table 2).

Thus, for the LR model MAE can be reduced by data augmentation by 0.01 (compare model 6 to 4) and by feature selection by an additional 0.04 (compare model 13 to 6). The accuracy improved by 3.5 percentage points.

**LLM prompting** We also experimented with *LLaMA* for this task. We tested its performance for a) annotating the number of statements, b) predicting the statement spans, and c) identifying whether a specific rule in the annotation guidelines applied to a sentence. An example of this is to predict whether the adjectives in this sentence constitute a new statement or not. This approach was primarily exploratory, but we still want to share our results. An example prompt can be found in Appendix B.

Out of all of these applications, LLMs worked best for predicting the number of statements with an accuracy of 66.83% on the test set. However, this accuracy is mainly due to *LLaMA* over predicting sentences with one statement. *LLaMA* struggled with predicting statement spans, presumably because this is a much more complex task, where a mistake in the first reasoning step easily leads to errors down the line. To test the individual rules in the annotation guidelines, we crafted a set of sentences and manually annotated whether the specific rule we wanted to test was true or not. Due to the manual nature of this part, we tested on a smaller set of samples for the annotation rules, so the results should be viewed as more of an initial investigation. Out of all the rules, LLMs seemed to perform well at deciding whether an adjective adds a new statement or not and moderately well for predicting zero statements. For the other rules, its predictions were hardly better than chance. With a fine-tuned model and larger example sets, results might increase. However, given the lower explainability of LLMs compared to our other methods and since their accuracy did not match that of our other approaches, we decided not to pursue this method further.

### 5.1.1 Submission

We extend the BERT architecture (refer Section 4.3) to incorporate part-of-speech (POS) information alongside the contextual embeddings generated by BERT. This model consists of three main components: a pre-trained German BERT model, a POS encoder that transforms POS tags into dense representations, and a classifier that combines BERT outputs with encoded POS features. By encoding POS tags, the model potentially gains access to extra syntactic knowledge that might not be fully captured in BERT's learned representations alone.

The model's forward pass begins by processing the input text through the BERT model to get the contextual embeddings. We then extract the [CLS] token representation from BERT's last hidden state. After that, we get the POS tags for each input text using the SpaCy *de_core_news_lg*[18] language model and encode the POS tags using a simple one-hot encoding. At the same time, the POS tags are encoded using a linear layer to create dense representations. The BERT [CLS] token representation and the encoded POS features are concatenated and passed through a final linear classifier to predict the number of statements. We use the Adam optimizer (Kingma and Ba, 2014) with a learning rate of 2e-5 and train the model for 100 epochs with a batch size of 16.

We combine the trial, train, and test datasets provided by the organizers (for details, see Section 3.2), remove zero-statement sentences, and get 2,937 samples. We split this dataset into 90% training and 10% test datasets by randomly shuffling the samples. In the end, the training set and test set consist of 2,643 and 294 samples, respectively. On this test set, the model achieved an accuracy of 80%.

On the evaluation dataset provided by the organizers, our model achieved a precision of 0.65, a recall of 0.68, and an F1-score of 0.65. In terms of prediction accuracy, the model achieved a Mean Absolute Error (MAE) of 0.36, indicating that, on average, our predictions deviate by approximately 0.36 units from the true values. The Mean Squared Error (MSE) is 0.43, which is slightly higher than MAE, but the difference (0.07) is quite low, which means our model is generally consistent and has very few large outliers in the predictions.

[18]`https://spacy.io/models/de`

## 5.2 Subtask 2: Annotating the statement spans

The goal of the task is to identify and annotate distinct statements within a sentence, particularly when a sentence contains multiple statements. We approach this sequence labeling problem as a token classification task. This approach allowed us to adapt the BERT model used for subtask 1 (see Section 5.1.1), which is already fine-tuned for statement-level classification, to perform token-level predictions. In this framework, we transform the original attention span labels into token-level classifications. We use the `tokenized phrase` provided in the dataset (see Section 3.2), and each token is assigned a label corresponding to its position within the statement span. For example, consider the `tokenized phrase`, ['Alcopop', 'ist', 'ein', 'süßes', 'Getränk.'] which has the attention span of [[0, 1, 4], [3]] and is converted to [1, 1, 0, 2, 1], since 'Alcopop', 'ist' and 'Getränk.' belongs to the first span (labeled as 1), 'ein' belongs to none of the spans (labeled as 0) and 'süßes' belongs to the second span (labeled as 2).

### 5.2.1 Submission

The fine-tuned BERT used for subtask 1 (refer Section 5.1.1) is further fine-tuned for this token classification task. This approach leverages transfer learning, allowing the model to build upon the knowledge gained from the broader statement-level classification to perform the more specific token-level classification. We modify the top layers of the already fine-tuned model by retaining the pre-trained BERT layers, adding a part-of-speech (POS) encoder to incorporate syntactic information, and implementing a new classification layer for token-level predictions.

In the forward pass, the model first processes the input (tokenized phrase) through BERT, obtaining the last hidden state. It then encodes the POS tags using the POS encoder. These two outputs are concatenated along the last dimension, combining contextual information from BERT with the POS information. Finally, this combined representation is passed through the classifier to produce logits for each token. The loss is computed on the flattened logits and labels, treating each token as an independent classification problem (padded tokens are ignored).

We then fine-tuned this adapted model on the evaluation dataset (provided by the organizers) following the same split as subtask 1 (90% train and

10% test split), but the sentences were shuffled. We use the Adam optimizer (Kingma and Ba, 2014) with a learning rate of 2e-5 and train the model for ten epochs with a batch size of 16.

Our model's performance was evaluated using two key metrics: chrF and Jaccard similarity. The chrF score indicates the model's ability to capture character-level n-gram similarities between the predicted and reference texts (Popović, 2015). The Jaccard similarity is a statistical measure used to gauge the similarity and diversity of sample sets. The model achieved a chrF score of 0.36 and a Jaccard similarity of 0.29 on the evaluation dataset provided by the organizers.

## 6 Conclusion and Future work

Our experiments focused on both detecting the number of statements and subsequently detecting the annotation spans of Simple German sentences, namely both subtasks 1 and 2 of the GermEval "Statement Segmentation in German Easy Language (StaGE)" shared task.

In subtask 1 of detecting the number of statements (Section 5.1), the submitted model that extended the BERT architecture by incorporating POS features scored a 0.65 precision, 0.68 recall, and 0.65 F1-score on the evaluation dataset. The Mean Absolute Error (MAE) and the Mean Squared Error (MSE) were 0.36 and 0.43, respectively. The relatively small difference between MAE and MSE suggests consistent performance without significant outliers.

For the Subtask 2 of statement span annotation (Section 5.1), we adapted the BERT model used for subtask 1 to perform token-level classification. This approach achieved a chrF score of 0.36 and a Jaccard similarity of 0.29. While these scores indicate room for improvement, they demonstrate the model's ability to identify and annotate distinct statements within a sentence.

These results provide encouraging evidence for the effectiveness of our approach, particularly using BERT with POS information for both subtasks. Moreover, our exploration of various methods, from rule-based systems to fine-tuning language models, allowed us to gain insights into the strengths and limitations of different approaches for both subtasks.

### 6.1 Future work

Based on the results and approach described, we would like to propose some potential directions for future work.

We would like to investigate a multi-task learning approach, where the model is trained simultaneously on both statement identification and span annotation tasks, which could provide an improved performance across both tasks by using shared linguistic knowledge.

We plan to compare the performance of our BERT architecture with other pre-trained language models like RoBERTa (Liu et al., 2019), XLNet (Yang et al., 2019) or T5 (Raffel et al., 2020) or mBART (Liu et al., 2020). This will help us identify the most effective base model for the given tasks. With regard to the *LLaMA* approach, it would be interesting to explore fine-tuned models and integrate the LLM's judgment with other approaches, for example, rule-based.

## Limitations

We acknowledge a few limitations in our approach. A significant limitation is that we did not perform hyperparameter tuning for our extended BERT model for both tasks. We focused on extending BERT but did not explore other pre-trained models. We did not conduct any analysis on how the POS information influences the model's decision. We did not conduct ablation studies to understand the individual contribution of different components of our model, such as the POS encoder or specific layers of our BERT architecture.

## Ethics Statement

We fully complied with all rules, guidelines, and data usage policies set forth by the shared task organizers. We accurately represented our models' capabilities and limitations. *LLaMA* was used solely for inference purposes; we did not fine-tune our model. We aimed to use computational resources efficiently by leveraging pre-trained models. Our submissions reflect our own work.

## CRediT authorship contribution statement

We follow the CRediT taxonomy[19]. Conceptualization: [AKR, ES, AS, HX, WP]; Formal Analysis: [AKR, ES, AS, HX, WP]; Investigation: [AKR, ES, AS, HX, WP]; Methodology: [AKR, AS, WP];

[19] `https://credit.niso.org/`

Supervision: [AKR, AS, WP]; and Writing – original draft: [AKR, ES, AS, HX, WP] and Writing – review & editing: [AKR, ES, AS, HX, WP].

## Acknowledgments

We thank the organizers of both subtasks for their effort and for their help during the training and evaluation phases. We would like to thank Nele Mastracchio for helping in the initial ideation phase of this project. We acknowledge the use of Google Colab[20] for providing some of the computational resources necessary for this research.

## References

Suha S Al-Thanyyan and Aqil M Azmi. 2021. Automated text simplification: a survey. *ACM Computing Surveys (CSUR)*, 54(2):1–36.

Fernando Alva-Manchego, Carolina Scarton, and Lucia Specia. 2021. The (Un)Suitability of Automatic Evaluation Metrics for Text Simplification. *Computational Linguistics*, 47(4):861–889.

David Arps, Jan Kels, Florian Krämer, Yunus Renz, Regina Stodden, and Wiebke Petersen. 2022. HHUplexity at text complexity DE challenge 2022. In *Proceedings of the GermEval 2022 Workshop on Text Complexity Assessment of German Text*, pages 27–32, Potsdam, Germany. Association for Computational Linguistics.

Hadi Asghari, Freya Hewett, and Theresa Züger. 2023. On the prevalence of leichte sprache on the german web. In *Proceedings of the 15th ACM Web Science Conference 2023*, pages 147–152.

Anthony Baez and Horacio Saggion. 2023. LSLlama: Fine-Tuned LLaMA for Lexical Simplification. In *Proceedings of the Second Workshop on Text Simplification, Accessibility and Readability*, pages 102–108, Varna, Bulgaria. INCOMA Ltd., Shoumen, Bulgaria.

Laura Banarescu, Claire Bonial, Shu Cai, Madalina Georgescu, Kira Griffitt, Ulf Hermjakob, Kevin Knight, Philipp Koehn, Martha Palmer, and Nathan Schneider. 2013. Abstract meaning representation for sembanking. In *LAW@ACL*.

Bettina M Bock. 2014. „leichte sprache“: Abgrenzung, beschreibung und problemstellungen aus sicht der linguistik. *Sprache barrierefrei gestalten. Perspektiven aus der Angewandten Linguistik*, pages 17–51.

Klaus Buddeberg and Anke Grotlüschen, editors. 2020. *LEO 2018: Leben mit geringer Literalität*. wbv Publikation, Bielefeld.

[20]`https://colab.research.google.com/`

Bundesministerium des Innern und für Heimat. 2011. Barrierefreie-informationstechnik-verordnung 2.0. `https://www.barrierefreiheit-dienstekonsolidierung.bund.de/Webs/PB/DE/gesetze-und-richtlinien/bitv2-0/bitv2-0-artikel.html`. accessed: 17.04.2024.

Raman Chandrasekar and Bangalore Srinivas. 1997. Automatic induction of rules for text simplification. *Knowledge-Based Systems*, 10(3):183–190.

Vittorio Ciccarelli, Cornelia Genz, Nele Mastracchio, Wiebke Petersen, Anna Stein, and Hanxin Xia. 2024. Team art-nat-HHU at SemEval-2024 task 8: Stylistically informed fusion model for MGT-detection. In *Proceedings of the 18th International Workshop on Semantic Evaluation (SemEval-2024)*, pages 1690–1697, Mexico City, Mexico. Association for Computational Linguistics.

Jacob Devlin, Ming-Wei Chang, Kenton Lee, and Kristina Toutanova. 2019. BERT: Pre-training of deep bidirectional transformers for language understanding. In *Proceedings of the 2019 Conference of the North American Chapter of the Association for Computational Linguistics: Human Language Technologies, Volume 1 (Long and Short Papers)*, pages 4171–4186, Minneapolis, Minnesota. Association for Computational Linguistics.

Sarah Ebling, Alessia Battisti, Marek Kostrzewa, Dominik Pfütze, Annette Rios, Andreas Säuberli, and Nicolas Spring. 2022. Automatic text simplification for german. *Frontiers in Communication*, 7:706718.

Annette Rios Gonzales, Nicolas Spring, Tannon Kew, Marek Kostrzewa, Andreas Säuberli, Mathias Müller, and Sarah Ebling. 2021. A new dataset and efficient baselines for document-level text simplification in german. In *Proceedings of the Third Workshop on New Frontiers in Summarization*, pages 152–161.

Matthew Honnibal and Ines Montani. 2020. spacy: Industrial-strength natural language processing in python.

Diederik P. Kingma and Jimmy Ba. 2014. Adam: A method for stochastic optimization. *CoRR*, abs/1412.6980.

Nikita Kitaev, Steven Cao, and Dan Klein. 2019. Multilingual constituency parsing with self-attention and pre-training. In *Proceedings of the 57th Annual Meeting of the Association for Computational Linguistics*, pages 3499–3505, Florence, Italy. Association for Computational Linguistics.

Nikita Kitaev and Dan Klein. 2018. Constituency parsing with a self-attentive encoder. In *Proceedings of the 56th Annual Meeting of the Association for Computational Linguistics (Volume 1: Long Papers)*, pages 2676–2686, Melbourne, Australia. Association for Computational Linguistics.

Irene Langkilde and Kevin Knight. 1998. Generation that exploits corpus-based statistical knowledge. In *COLING 1998 Volume 1: The 17th International Conference on Computational Linguistics*.

Yinhan Liu, Jiatao Gu, Naman Goyal, Xian Li, Sergey Edunov, Marjan Ghazvininejad, Mike Lewis, and Luke Zettlemoyer. 2020. Multilingual denoising pre-training for neural machine translation. *Transactions of the Association for Computational Linguistics*, 8:726–742.

Yinhan Liu, Myle Ott, Naman Goyal, Jingfei Du, Mandar Joshi, Danqi Chen, Omer Levy, Mike Lewis, Luke Zettlemoyer, and Veselin Stoyanov. 2019. Roberta: A robustly optimized bert pretraining approach. *ArXiv*, abs/1907.11692.

Christiane Maaß and Ursula Bredel. 2017. *Ratgeber Leichte Sprache: Die wichtigsten Regeln und Empfehlungen für die Praxis*. Duden. ISBN: 9783411912360.

Jonathan Mallinson, Rico Sennrich, and Mirella Lapata. 2020. Zero-shot crosslingual sentence simplification. In *Proceedings of the 2020 Conference on Empirical Methods in Natural Language Processing (EMNLP)*, pages 5109–5126, Online. Association for Computational Linguistics.

Christina Niklaus, Matthias Cetto, André Freitas, and Siegfried Handschuh. 2019. DisSim: A discourse-aware syntactic text simplification framework for English and German. In *Proceedings of the 12th International Conference on Natural Language Generation*, pages 504–507, Tokyo, Japan. Association for Computational Linguistics.

Fabian Pedregosa, Gaël Varoquaux, Alexandre Gramfort, Vincent Michel, Bertrand Thirion, Olivier Grisel, Mathieu Blondel, Peter Prettenhofer, Ron Weiss, Vincent Dubourg, et al. 2011. Scikit-learn: Machine learning in python. *Journal of machine learning research*, 12(Oct):2825–2830. Ver. 1.5.0.

Maja Popović. 2015. chrf: character n-gram f-score for automatic mt evaluation. In *Proceedings of the tenth workshop on statistical machine translation*, pages 392–395.

Colin Raffel, Noam Shazeer, Adam Roberts, Katherine Lee, Sharan Narang, Michael Matena, Yanqi Zhou, Wei Li, and Peter J Liu. 2020. Exploring the limits of transfer learning with a unified text-to-text transformer. *Journal of machine learning research*, 21(140):1–67.

Michael Ryan, Tarek Naous, and Wei Xu. 2023. Revisiting non-English text simplification: A unified multilingual benchmark. In *Proceedings of the 61st Annual Meeting of the Association for Computational Linguistics (Volume 1: Long Papers)*, pages 4898–4927, Toronto, Canada. Association for Computational Linguistics.

Andreas Säuberli, Sarah Ebling, and Martin Volk. 2020. Benchmarking data-driven automatic text simplification for German. In *Proceedings of the 1st Workshop on Tools and Resources to Empower People with REAding DIfficulties (READI)*, pages 41–48, Marseille, France. European Language Resources Association.

Teven Le Scao, Angela Fan, Christopher Akiki, Ellie Pavlick, Suzana Ilić, Daniel Hesslow, Roman Castagné, Alexandra Sasha Luccioni, François Yvon, Matthias Gallé, Jonathan Tow, Alexander M. Rush, Stella Biderman, Albert Webson, Pawan Sasanka Ammanamanchi, Thomas Wang, Benoît Sagot, Niklas Muennighoff, Albert Villanova del Moral, Olatunji Ruwase, Rachel Bawden, Stas Bekman, Angelina Mcmillan-Major, Iz Beltagy, Huu Nguyen, Lucile Saulnier, Samson Tan, Pedro Ortiz Suarez, Victor Sanh, Hugo Laurençon, Yacine Jernite, Julien Launay, Margaret Mitchell, Colin Raffel, Aaron Gokaslan, Adi Simhi, Aitor Soroa, Alham Fikri Aji, Amit Alfassy, Anna Rogers, Ariel Kreisberg Nitzav, Canwen Xu, Chenghao Mou, Chris Emezue, Christopher Klamm, Colin Leong, Daniel van Strien, David Ifeoluwa Adelani, Dragomir Radev, Eduardo González Ponferrada, Efrat Levkovizh, Ethan Kim, Eyal Bar Natan, Francesco de Toni, Gérard Dupont, Germán Kruszewski, Giada Pistilli, Hady Elsahar, Hamza Benyamina, Hieu Tran, Ian Yu, Idris Abdulmumin, Isaac Johnson, Itziar Gonzalez-Dios, Javier de la Rosa, Jenny Chim, Jesse Dodge, Jian Zhu, Jonathan Chang, Jörg Frohberg, Joseph Tobing, Joydeep Bhattacharjee, Khalid Almubarak, Kimbo Chen, Kyle Lo, Leandro von Werra, Leon Weber, Long Phan, Loubna Ben Allal, Ludovic Tanguy, Manan Dey, Manuel Romero Muñoz, Maraim Masoud, María Grandury, Mario Šaško, Max Huang, Maximin Coavoux, Mayank Singh, Mike Tian-Jian Jiang, Minh Chien Vu, Mohammad A. Jauhar, Mustafa Ghaleb, Nishant Subramani, Nora Kassner, Nurulaqilla Khamis, Olivier Nguyen, Omar Espejel, Ona de Gibert, Paulo Villegas, Peter Henderson, Pierre Colombo, Priscilla Amuok, Quentin Lhoest, Rheza Harliman, Rishi Bommasani, Roberto Luis López, Rui Ribeiro, Salomey Osei, Sampo Pyysalo, Sebastian Nagel, Shamik Bose, Shamsuddeen Hassan Muhammad, Shanya Sharma, Shayne Longpre, Somaieh Nikpoor, Stanislav Silberberg, Suhas Pai, Sydney Zink, Tiago Timponi Torrent, Timo Schick, Tristan Thrush, Valentin Danchev, Vassilina Nikoulina, Veronika Laippala, Violette Lepercq, Vrinda Prabhu, Zaid Alyafeai, Zeerak Talat, Arun Raja, Benjamin Heinzerling, Chenglei Si, Elizabeth Salesky, Sabrina J. Mielke, Wilson Y. Lee, Abheesht Sharma, Andrea Santilli, Antoine Chaffin, Arnaud Stiegler, Debajyoti Datta, Eliza Szczechla, Gunjan Chhablani, Han Wang, Harshit Pandey, Hendrik Strobelt, Jason Alan Fries, Jos Rozen, Leo Gao, Lintang Sutawika, M Saiful Bari, Maged S. Al-Shaibani, Matteo Manica, Nihal Nayak, Ryan Teehan, Samuel Albanie, Sheng Shen, Srulik Ben-David, Stephen H. Bach, Taewoon Kim, Tali Bers, Thibault Fevry, Trishala Neeraj, Urmish Thakker, Vikas Raunak, Xiangru Tang, Zheng-Xin Yong, Zhiqing Sun, Shaked Brody, Yallow Uri,

Hadar Tojarieh, Adam Roberts, Hyung Won Chung, Jaesung Tae, Jason Phang, Ofir Press, Conglong Li, Deepak Narayanan, Hatim Bourfoune, Jared Casper, Jeff Rasley, Max Ryabinin, Mayank Mishra, Minjia Zhang, Mohammad Shoeybi, Myriam Peyrounette, Nicolas Patry, Nouamane Tazi, Omar Sanseviero, Patrick von Platen, Pierre Cornette, Pierre François Lavallée, Rémi Lacroix, Samyam Rajbhandari, Sanchit Gandhi, Shaden Smith, Stéphane Requena, Suraj Patil, Tim Dettmers, Ahmed Baruwa, Amanpreet Singh, Anastasia Cheveleva, Anne-Laure Ligozat, Arjun Subramonian, Aurélie Névéol, Charles Lovering, Dan Garrette, Deepak Tunuguntla, Ehud Reiter, Ekaterina Taktasheva, Ekaterina Voloshina, Eli Bogdanov, Genta Indra Winata, Hailey Schoelkopf, Jan-Christoph Kalo, Jekaterina Novikova, Jessica Zosa Forde, Jordan Clive, Jungo Kasai, Ken Kawamura, Liam Hazan, Marine Carpuat, Miruna Clinciu, Najoung Kim, Newton Cheng, Oleg Serikov, Omer Antverg, Oskar van der Wal, Rui Zhang, Ruochen Zhang, Sebastian Gehrmann, Shani Pais, Tatiana Shavrina, Thomas Scialom, Tian Yun, Tomasz Limisiewicz, Verena Rieser, Vitaly Protasov, Vladislav Mikhailov, Yada Pruksachatkun, Yonatan Belinkov, Zachary Bamberger, Zdeněk Kasner, Alice Rueda, Amanda Pestana, Amir Feizpour, Ammar Khan, Amy Faranak, Ana Santos, Anthony Hevia, Antigona Unldreaj, Arash Aghagol, Arezoo Abdollahi, Aycha Tammour, Azadeh Hajihosseini, Bahareh Behroozi, Benjamin Ajibade, Bharat Saxena, Carlos Muñoz Ferrandis, Danish Contractor, David Lansky, Davis David, Douwe Kiela, Duong A. Nguyen, Edward Tan, Emi Baylor, Ezinwanne Ozoani, Fatima Mirza, Frankline Ononiwu, Habib Rezanejad, Hessie Jones, Indrani Bhattacharya, Irene Solaiman, Irina Sedenko, Isar Nejadgholi, Jesse Passmore, Josh Seltzer, Julio Bonis Sanz, Livia Dutra, Mairon Samagaio, Maraim Elbadri, Margot Mieskes, Marissa Gerchick, Martha Akinlolu, Michael Mckenna, Mike Qiu, Muhammed Ghauri, Mykola Burynok, Nafis Abrar, Nazneen Rajani, Nour Elkott, Nour Fahmy, Olanrewaju Samuel, Ran An, Rasmus Kromann, Ryan Hao, Samira Alizadeh, Sarmad Shubber, Silas Wang, Sourav Roy, Sylvain Viguier, Thanh Le, Tobi Oyebade, Trieu Le, Yoyo Yang, Zach Nguyen, Abhinav Ramesh Kashyap, Alfredo Palasciano, Alison Callahan, Anima Shukla, Antonio Miranda-Escalada, Ayush Singh, Benjamin Beilharz, Bo Wang, Caio Brito, Chenxi Zhou, Chirag Jain, Chuxin Xu, Clémentine Fourrier, Daniel León Periñán, Daniel Molano, Dian Yu, Enrique Manjavacas, Fabio Barth, Florian Fuhrimann, Gabriel Altay, Giyaseddin Bayrak, Gully Burns, Helena U. Vrabec, Imane Bello, Ishani Dash, Jihyun Kang, John Giorgi, Jonas Golde, Jose David Posada, Karthik Rangasai Sivaraman, Lokesh Bulchandani, Lu Liu, Luisa Shinzato, Madeleine Hahn de Bykhovetz, Maiko Takeuchi, Marc Pàmies, Maria A Castillo, Marianna Nezhurina, Mario Sänger, Matthias Samwald, Michael Cullan, Michael Weinberg, Michiel de Wolf, Mina Mihaljcic, Minna Liu, Moritz Freidank, Myungsun Kang, Natasha Seelam, Nathan Dahlberg, Nicholas Michio Broad, Nikolaus Muellner, Pascale Fung, Patrick Haller, Ramya Chandrasekhar, Renata Eisenberg, Robert Martin, Rodrigo Canalli, Rosaline Su, Ruisi Su, Samuel Cahyawijaya, Samuele Garda, Shlok S Deshmukh, Shubhanshu Mishra, Sid Kiblawi, Simon Ott, Sinee Sang-Aroonsiri, Srishti Kumar, Stefan Schweter, Sushil Bharati, Tanmay Laud, Théo Gigant, Tomoya Kainuma, Wojciech Kusa, Yanis Labrak, Yash Shailesh Bajaj, Yash Venkatraman, Yifan Xu, Yingxin Xu, Yu Xu, Zhe Tan, Zhongli Xie, Zifan Ye, Mathilde Bras, Younes Belkada, and Thomas Wolf. 2023. BLOOM: A 176B-Parameter Open-Access Multilingual Language Model. Working paper or preprint.

Thorben Schomacker, Miriam Anschütz, Regina Stodden, Marina Tropmann-Frick, and Georg Groh. 2024. Overview of the germeval 2024 shared task on statement segmentation in german easy language (stage). In *Proceedings of the GermEval 2024 Shared Task on Statement Segmentation in German Easy Language (StaGE)*, Vienna, Austria. Association for Computational Linguistics.

Thorben Schomacker, Tillmann Dönicke, and Marina Tropmann-Frick. 2023. Exploring automatic text simplification of German narrative documents. In *Proceedings of the 19th Conference on Natural Language Processing (KONVENS 2023)*, pages 139–148, Ingolstadt, Germany. Association for Computational Lingustics.

Matthew Shardlow. 2014. A survey of automated text simplification. *International Journal of Advanced Computer Science and Applications*, 4(1):58–70.

Melanie Siegel, Dorothee Beermann, and Lars Hellan. 2019. Aspects of linguistic complexity: A german – norwegian approach to the creation of resources for easy-to-understand language. In *2019 Eleventh International Conference on Quality of Multimedia Experience (QoMEX)*, pages 1–3.

Nicolas Spring, Annette Rios, and Sarah Ebling. 2021. Exploring German multi-level text simplification. In *Proceedings of the International Conference on Recent Advances in Natural Language Processing (RANLP 2021)*, pages 1339–1349, Held Online. INCOMA Ltd.

Ina Steinmetz and Karin Harbusch. 2022. A text-writing system for easy-to-read German evaluated with low-literate users with cognitive impairment. In *Proceedings of the First Workshop on Intelligent and Interactive Writing Assistants (In2Writing 2022)*, pages 27–38, Dublin, Ireland. Association for Computational Linguistics.

Regina Stodden. 2024. Reproduction of German text simplification systems. In *Proceedings of the Workshop on DeTermIt! Evaluating Text Difficulty in a Multilingual Context @ LREC-COLING 2024*, pages 1–15, Torino, Italia. ELRA and ICCL.

Julia Suter, Sarah Ebling, and Martin Volk. 2016. Rule-based automatic text simplification for german. In *Proceedings of the 13th Conference on Natural*

*Language Processing, KONVENS 2016, Bochum, Germany, September 19-21, 2016*, volume 16 of *Bochumer Linguistische Arbeitsberichte*.

Keren Tan, Kangyang Luo, Yunshi Lan, Zheng Yuan, and Jinlong Shu. 2024. An llm-enhanced adversarial editing system for lexical simplification. *Preprint*, arXiv:2402.14704.

Vanessa Toborek, Moritz Busch, Malte Boßert, Christian Bauckhage, and Pascal Welke. 2023. A new aligned simple German corpus. In *Proceedings of the 61st Annual Meeting of the Association for Computational Linguistics (Volume 1: Long Papers)*, pages 11393–11412, Toronto, Canada. Association for Computational Linguistics.

Ashish Vaswani, Noam Shazeer, Niki Parmar, Jakob Uszkoreit, Llion Jones, Aidan N Gomez, Łukasz Kaiser, and Illia Polosukhin. 2017. Attention is all you need. *Advances in neural information processing systems*, 30.

Jason Wei, Xuezhi Wang, Dale Schuurmans, Maarten Bosma, brian ichter, Fei Xia, Ed Chi, Quoc V Le, and Denny Zhou. 2022. Chain-of-thought prompting elicits reasoning in large language models. In *Advances in Neural Information Processing Systems*, volume 35, pages 24824–24837. Curran Associates, Inc.

Zhilin Yang, Zihang Dai, Yiming Yang, Jaime Carbonell, Russ R Salakhutdinov, and Quoc V Le. 2019. Xlnet: Generalized autoregressive pretraining for language understanding. *Advances in neural information processing systems*, 32.

Zhuosheng Zhang, Aston Zhang, Mu Li, and Alex Smola. 2022. Automatic Chain of Thought Prompting in Large Language Models. *arXiv preprint*. ArXiv:2210.03493 [cs] version: 1.

# Appendix

## A Extracted Features

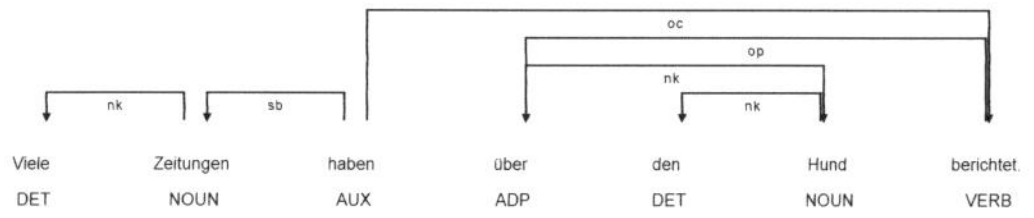


Figure 1: Dependency tree of phrase 'Viele Zeitungen haben über den Hund berichtet.' The following features are extracted from this tree: 'max_dep_length', 'mean_dep_length', 'min_dep_length', 'num_dep_paths', 'num_root', 'num_root_childs', 'oc#', 'oc#op#', 'oc#op#nk#', 'oc#op#nk#nk#', 'oc#op#nk#nk#DET', 'punct#', 'punct#PUNCT', 'sb#', 'sb#nk#', 'sb#nk#DET'

```
(r / report-01
      :ARG0 (n / newspaper
            :quant (m / many))
      :ARG1 (d / dog))
```

Figure 2: AMR of phrase 'Many newspapers have reported about the dog.' The following features are extracted from this AMR: 'arg0:', 'arg0:instance:', 'arg0:quant:', 'arg0:quant:instance:', 'arg0:quant:instance:many', 'arg1:', 'arg1:instance:', 'instance:'

```
((S
  (ADV Leider)
  (VVFIN bekomme)
  (PPER ich)
  (NP (PIAT keine) (NN Katze)))
($, ,))
```

Figure 3: An example of NLTK tree forms

## B LLM prompts

The following is an example of an LLM prompt we used. Text in **bold** was not part of the prompt but is included here to illustrate the different prompt levels. For the sake of clarity, the prompt is slightly shortened, the full prompt can be found in our GitHub repository.

**System prompt**
You are an expert in German Easy Language.
**User prompt**
Give the statement spans of the sentence below.
For your decisions rely on the annotation guidelines provided below. Provide your output in the form of a nested list. Return nothing but that list or the string "None" if the sentence only has one statement or zero statements.
Think step by step.
Three example sentences:
sentence: Eine sehr bekannte Alchemisten war Maria die Jüdin
statements: 1, statement spans: None;
(We provided two more examples but did not include them here for the sake of brevity.)

The sentence you should annotate is the following:
{sentence}
Annotation guidelines:
{annotation_guidelines}

## C Feature Importance

| Features | Importance |
|---|---|
| attr-arg1:attr-instance: | 0.0088 |
| amr_length | 0.0084 |
| attr-arg1: | 0.0083 |
| attr-arg2: | 0.0077 |
| attr-arg0:attr-instance: | 0.0076 |
| attr-arg2:attr-instance: | 0.0075 |
| attr-(mod):attr-instance: | 0.0074 |
| attr-(mod): | 0.0074 |
| attr-arg0: | 0.0073 |
| attr-time:attr-instance: | 0.0071 |

Table 3: Ranked 10 most important AMR-features

| Feature | Importance |
|---|---|
| max_dep_length | 0.1012 |
| mean_dep_length | 0.0869 |
| num_dep_paths | 0.0787 |
| num_root_childs | 0.0523 |
| sb#PRON | 0.0137 |
| sb#nk#DET | 0.0134 |
| sb#nk# | 0.0123 |
| mo#ADV | 0.0108 |
| num_root | 0.0101 |
| oa# | 0.0089 |

Table 4: Ranked 10 most important dependency tree features

| Feature | Importance |
|---|---|
| token_count | 0.1738 |
| mean_chars_per_word | 0.0956 |
| wiener_sachtextformel | 0.0946 |
| flesch_reading_ease | 0.0814 |
| num_compound | 0.0725 |
| num_nouns | 0.0584 |
| verb_count | 0.0472 |
| num_PP | 0.0464 |
| class_score | 0.0395 |
| num_S | 0.0381 |

Table 5: Ranked 10 most important additional linguistic features

| Feature | Importance |
|---|---|
| token_count | 0.06 |
| max_dep_length | 0.0328 |
| num_dep_paths | 0.0328 |
| mean_dep_length | 0.0256 |
| num_compound | 0.0211 |
| UMAP2 | 0.0179 |
| UMAP4 | 0.0176 |
| UMAP1 | 0.0176 |
| UMAP0 | 0.0168 |
| UMAP8 | 0.0166 |
| UMAP9 | 0.0161 |
| UMAP5 | 0.0161 |
| UMAP7 | 0.016 |
| verb_count | 0.016 |
| UMAP3 | 0.0158 |
| flesch_reading_ease | 0.0155 |
| num_S | 0.0154 |
| wiener_sachtextformel | 0.0153 |
| UMAP6 | 0.0146 |
| mean_chars_per_word | 0.0146 |

Table 6: Ranked 20 most important features (over all feature classes)

# Statement Segmentation for German Easy Language Using BERT and Dependency Parsing

**Andreas Säuberli***
Department of Computational Linguistics
University of Zurich
andreas.saeuberli@uzh.ch

**Niclas Bodenmann***
Independent researcher
niclas.bodenmann@gmx.ch

## Abstract

Texts in Easy Language should contain a low number of statements per sentence, to make information more accessible and comprehensible. The shared task *Statement Segmentation in German Easy Language (StaGE)* aims to automatically identify the number and location of statements in German Easy Language sentences. We present our submission to this task, which combines sequence labeling with dependency parsing. Our approach uses a fine-tuned BERT model to predict the head token of each statement span and expands the span using dependency relations. Our model achieves a mean absolute error of 0.40 in the predicted number of statements and Jaccard index of 0.38 in the statement spans. We discuss the challenges and limitations of the task and outline future research directions.

## 1 Introduction

Easy Language is a simplified variety of language with the goal of improving information accessibility, e.g., for persons with cognitive disabilities, prelingual hearing impairments, dementia, or aphasia (Maaß, 2020). The draft for DIN SPEC 33429 (DIN, 2023) represents a recent attempt to provide a standardized set of recommendations and guidelines for creating content in German Easy Language. One of these recommendations is that sentences in Easy Language should contain a small number of statements (DIN, 2023, p. 14). While the document does not elaborate on a specific definition of the term *statement*, this has prompted the conception of the shared task on *Statement Segmentation in German Easy Language (StaGE)*[1] (Schomacker et al., 2024). The aim of the shared task is to automatically identify and segment statements in German Easy Language sentences.

This paper describes our submission to the shared task under the team name *StaGE FriGHt*.

## 2 Tasks, data, and evaluation

The *StaGE* shared task comprises two subtasks:

**Subtask 1:** Predict the number of statements in a given sentence.

**Subtask 2:** If there is more than one statement in a sentence, identify the corresponding token spans for each statement.

The shared task defines *statements* in the theoretical framework of valency grammar, which posits that verbs carry obligatory slots that need to be filled in order to form sound sentences. If only the obligatory slots are filled, the sentence only contains one statement. For example, the sentence *She gave him a gift* contains one statement, because only the three obligatory slots of the verb *gave* are filled: the subject *she*, the direct object *a gift*, and the indirect object *him*.

Each additional, optional slot amounts to another statement. Moreover, optional noun modifiers such as adjectives are also considered to be separate statements. For example, the sentence *She gave him a beautiful gift for his birthday* contains three statements: the verb with its obligatory slots (*She gave him a gift*), the optional slot *for his birthday*, and the adjective *beautiful*. In Subtask 2, the goal is to identify the set of tokens that form each statement. Some function words such as articles or conjunctions are not considered part of the statement span.

The training data consists of 2944 manually annotated sentences. A development set with 416 sentences is provided. The test set contains 878

*Both authors contributed equally. The author order was randomized: https://www.aeaweb.org/journals/policies/random-author-order/search?RandomAuthorsSearch%5Bsearch%5D=rHNaKZoddapX

[1] https://german-easy-to-read.github.io/statements/

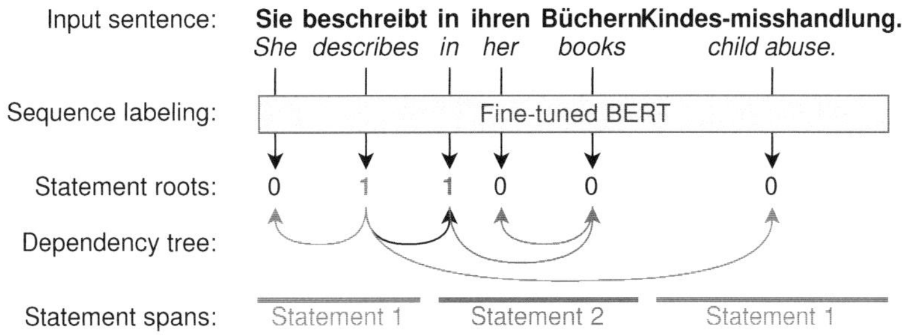


Figure 1: Our approach combines sequence labeling with dependency parsing: First, we use a fine-tuned BERT model to tag the head token of each statement span. We then apply dependency parsing and expand the spans to include all tokens that are dependent on the head token, while avoiding span overlap.

sentences. The data is available on GitHub.[2]

Subtask 1 is evaluated according to the mean absolute error (MAE) in the predicted number of statements. The spans extracted in Subtask 2 are evaluated using character-based F-score (chrF) and Jaccard index.

## 3 Sequence labeling for discontinuous span segmentation

From a technical perspective, one of the main challenges is that many of the provided statement spans are discontinuous. This means that well-established tagging formats such as the BIO format (Ramshaw and Marcus, 1995), which use a separate label for the beginning of each span, cannot be applied. Previously, several works have extended the BIO format with additional tags to accommodate discontinuous spans (Muis and Lu, 2016; Metke-Jimenez and Karimi, 2016; Tang et al., 2018) or resorted to multilabel classification (McDonald et al., 2005; Tang et al., 2018), adding considerable complexity to the task.

In some cases, spans in the dataset are also overlapping, but it is unclear what guidelines are applied. Compare the two following examples from the training set, both of which use similar syntactic constructions, but only one uses overlapping spans:

(1) *Durch Altenburg fließt der Fluss Pleisse.*
'The river Pleisse flows through Altenburg.'
Statements: [*Durch Altenburg* 'through Altenburg'], [*fließt Fluss* 'flows river'], [*fließt Pleisse.* 'flows Pleisse']

(2) *Sie ist Mitglied in der Partei Die Grünen*
'She is a member of the party The Greens.'
Statements: [*in Partei* 'in party'], [*Die Grünen* 'The Greens']

For simplicity, we restrict ourselves to predicting non-overlapping spans.

Since the statement spans often correspond to syntactical units such as clauses or prepositional phrases, we use syntactic dependency relations to construct statement spans. This allows us to frame the problem as a binary sequence labeling task, simplifying the tagging format compared to previous approaches. It also means that we can handle the two tasks of finding the statements and segmenting the sentence into spans separately.

Specifically, our approach involves the following steps (visualized in Figure 1):

1. We use a fine-tuned BERT model (Devlin et al., 2019) for sequence labeling, classifying for each token in the input sentence whether it is the head of a statement span (i.e., the highest-level token in the dependency hierarchy within that span).
2. We apply dependency parsing using *spaCy* (Honnibal et al., 2020) with the model `de_dep_news_trf`[3] to the input sentence and align the result to the tokenization in the dataset.
3. For each head token we found in step 1 (starting with the lowest-level one in the dependency tree), we expand the statement span around it by following the dependency relations, adding each descendant token to the span. We stop as soon as we reach a token that already belongs to a different span, to avoid overlap. We exclude articles, punctuation, and coordinating conjunctions.

[2] https://github.com/german-easy-to-read/statements/tree/master/data

[3] https://spacy.io/models/de#de_dep_news_trf

| Description | Sentence | True spans | Predicted spans |
|---|---|---|---|
| Correct | *Im Jahr 2002 macht Lula wieder mit bei der Prösidenten-wahl.* (sic) | [*Im Jahr 2002*] [*macht Lula wieder mit bei Prösidenten-wahl.*] | [*Im Jahr 2002*] [*macht Lula wieder mit bei Prösidenten-wahl.*] |
| (Translation:) | *In the year 2002, Lula is participating in the presidential election again.* | [*In year 2002,*] [*Lula is participating in presidential election again.*] | [*In year 2002,*] [*Lula is participating in presidential election again.*] |
| Missed span | Zum Beispiel kann man einen kleinen Text besser lesen. | [*Zum Beispiel kann man besser lesen.*] [*kleinen*] | (only one statement predicted) |
| (Translation:) | For example, you can read a small text better. | [*For example, you can read better.*] [*small*] | (only one statement predicted) |
| Excessive tagging | Ein Lurker schreibt selbst keine Artikel in einem Wiki. | [*Lurker schreibt selbst keine Artikel*] [*in Wiki.*] | [*Lurker schreibt selbst*] [*Artikel*] [*in*] [*Wiki.*] |
| (Translation:) | A lurker does not write articles in a wiki. | [*lurker does not write articles*] [*in wiki.*] | [*lurker writes*] [*articles*] [*in*] [*wiki.*] |
| Different segmentation | Seit dem Jahr 1983 gibt es Musik Alben von Madonna. | [*Seit Jahr 1983*] [*gibt es Musik Alben*] [*Musik Alben von Madonna*] | [*Seit Jahr 1983*] [*gibt es Musik Alben von*] [Madonna] |
| (Translation:) | There have been music albums by Madonna since the year 1983. | [*since year 1983.*] [*There have been music albums*] [*music albums by Madonna*] | [*since year 1983.*] [*There have been music albums by*] [Madonna] |

Table 1: Example predictions from the development set by our submitted model.

Preliminary experiments with several pre-trained German and multilingual BERT models suggested that the two models `bert-base-german-cased`[4] and `bert-base-multilingual-cased`[5] on the Hugging Face Hub are promising candidates for fine-tuning. We used these two models and performed grid search to optimize hyperparameters such as the number of epochs and batch size. We used span-level F1 score on the development set to determine the best-performing model to submit to the shared task. The code for data preprocessing, model fine-tuning, and the span expansion algorithm is available on GitHub.[6]

| Team | Subtask 1 MAE ↓ | Subtask 2 chrF ↑ | Jaccard ↑ |
|---|---|---|---|
| KlarTextCoder | **0.35** | **0.36** | 0.29 |
| CUET_Big_O | 0.40 | — | — |
| (Ours) | 0.40 | 0.30 | **0.38** |
| All-1 baseline | 0.66 | — | — |
| Random baseline | 0.92 | 0.24 | 0.27 |
| Conjunction baseline | 0.60 | 0.05 | 0.04 |

Table 2: Test set results of all participating teams and baselines provided by the organizers. Best score for each metric is in bold.

## 4 Results

The best-performing model that emerged from our grid search is based on the multilingually pre-trained BERT with an F1 score of 0.457, clearly outperforming the best German-based BERT model (F1: 0.416). We published our final model on the Hugging Face Hub for reproducibility.[7]

Table 2 shows results on the test set compared to the two other participating teams as well as three baselines provided by the organizers. The all-1 baseline predicts exactly one statement for each sentence. The random baseline predicts a random number of statements between one and three and splits sentences into spans of equal length. The conjunction baseline splits sentences at coordinating conjunctions such as *und* 'and' or *aber* 'but'.

The examples in Table 1 demonstrate that the model is capable of correctly distinguishing between optional and obligatory slots in many cases, but sometimes misses or overgenerates statements. Slight differences in segmentation often arise when the true annotation contains overlapping spans. Overall, the span expansion algorithm appears to work well in most cases.

[4]`https://huggingface.co/google-bert/bert-base-german-cased`

[5]`https://huggingface.co/google-bert/bert-base-multilingual-cased`

[6]`https://github.com/saeub/statement-segmentation`

[7]`https://huggingface.co/saeub/bert-stage`

## 5 Discussion

Our approach of only tagging a single token per statement and expanding spans by tracing downward dependencies has several advantages. The abstraction of the task as binary sequence labeling permits a more straightforward implementation compared to previous approaches for discontinuous spans. Separating span identification from span expansion allows a more modular development and granular evalution than end-to-end systems would. For example, it may be possible to adapt the rules in our span expansion algorithm to match the true spans even more closely without retraining the model.

However, the practical benefit of such overly specific optimizations towards exact span expansions is questionable. From an applied perspective, i.e., as part of the writing process, it might be more important to know which semantically central tokens (i.e., span heads) constitute additional statements, as opposed to know whether some preposition or particle belongs to a statement or not.

We would also like to critically put into question the definition of *statement* in terms of valency grammar. Realistic use cases for the statement segmentation task include computer-assisted translation into Easy Language and quality estimation of simplified texts, e.g., by pointing out sentences that should be split into several sentences. However, given the definition in the shared task, splitting the statements into separate sentences substantially changes the meaning in some cases. Consider this sentence from the training set:

(3) *Und man soll auch nicht allein Alkohol trinken.*
'And you shouldn't drink alcohol alone either.'
Statements: [*man soll auch nicht Alkohol trinken.* 'you shouldn't drink alcohol either.'], [*allein* 'alone']

Although syntactically optional, the adverbial *allein* is a crucial modifier of the recommendation not to drink alcohol, limiting its scope to a specific social context. While a grammatical view on *statement* may be easier to define, annotate, and automatically predict, it falls short when considering the semantic content and pragmatic context of the sentences.

## 6 Conclusion and future work

We presented our submission to the *StaGE* shared task on statement segmentation in German Easy Language. Our approach involves reframing the task as binary sequence labeling and reconstructing spans with a simple rule-based algorithm based on dependency relations. Among three teams, we achieved second place in terms of MAE in Subtask 1 and first place in terms of Jaccard index in Subtask 2.

Our results demonstrate that even generalist BERT models can achieve acceptable performance in emerging tasks in Easy Language. Future work might assess BERT models that are specifically pre-trained on Easy Language data. Anschütz et al. (2023) pre-trained GPT-based models on Easy Language, but to the best of our knowledge, no pre-trained masked language models exist for simplified language varieties. Another line of research could be to investigate alternative, more semantically and pragmatically motivated definitions of *statement*.

## Ethical considerations

Easy Language is an important contribution towards more inclusivity and accessibility in society. Research into Easy Language and technology that facilitates the creation of content in Easy Language is essential in this effort. However, it is important to acknowledge that users of Easy Language have diverse needs and requirements, and the effectiveness of guidelines and technologies should always be tested with target users. The *StaGE* shared task and our work focused solely on automatic evaluation metrics, which may not capture this effectiveness well. Therefore, we advise caution when interpreting the results in this paper and encourage future research to investigate the effectiveness of statement segmentation in the creation or evaluation of content in Easy Language.

## Acknowledgments

We would like to thank the StaGE organizers for providing the data and organizing the shared task, and the anonymous reviewers for their constructive feedback. We thank the Department of Computational Linguistics at the University of Zurich for providing the computational resources for our experiments.

## References


Miriam Anschütz, Joshua Oehms, Thomas Wimmer, Bartłomiej Jezierski, and Georg Groh. 2023. Language models for German text simplification: Overcoming parallel data scarcity through style-specific pre-training. In *Findings of the Association for Computational Linguistics: ACL 2023*, pages 1147–1158, Toronto, Canada. Association for Computational Linguistics.

Jacob Devlin, Ming-Wei Chang, Kenton Lee, and Kristina Toutanova. 2019. BERT: Pre-training of deep bidirectional transformers for language understanding. In *Proceedings of the 2019 Conference of the North American Chapter of the Association for Computational Linguistics: Human Language Technologies, Volume 1 (Long and Short Papers)*, pages 4171–4186, Minneapolis, Minnesota. Association for Computational Linguistics.

DIN. 2023. Empfehlungen für Deutsche Leichte Sprache (DIN SPEC 33429). Technical report, Deutsches Institut für Normierung e.V.

Matthew Honnibal, Ines Montani, Sofie Van Landeghem, and Adriane Boyd. 2020. spacy: Industrial-strength natural language processing in python. *Zenodo*. If you use spaCy, please cite it as below.

Christiane Maaß. 2020. *Easy Language–Plain Language–Easy Language Plus: Balancing comprehensibility and acceptability*. Frank & Timme, Berlin.

Ryan McDonald, Koby Crammer, and Fernando Pereira. 2005. Flexible text segmentation with structured multilabel classification. In *Proceedings of Human Language Technology Conference and Conference on Empirical Methods in Natural Language Processing*, pages 987–994, Vancouver, British Columbia, Canada. Association for Computational Linguistics.

Alejandro Metke-Jimenez and Sarvnaz Karimi. 2016. Concept identification and normalisation for adverse drug event discovery in medical forums. In *Proceedings of the First International Workshop on Biomedical Data Integration and Discovery (BMDID 2016)*.

Aldrian Obaja Muis and Wei Lu. 2016. Learning to recognize discontiguous entities. In *Proceedings of the 2016 Conference on Empirical Methods in Natural Language Processing*, pages 75–84, Austin, Texas. Association for Computational Linguistics.

Lance Ramshaw and Mitch Marcus. 1995. Text chunking using transformation-based learning. In *Third Workshop on Very Large Corpora*.

Thorben Schomacker, Miriam Anschütz, Regina Stodden, Marina Tropmann-Frick, and Georg Groh. 2024. Overview of the GermEval 2024 Shared Task on Statement Segmentation in German Easy Language (StaGE). In *Proceedings of the GermEval 2024 Shared Task on Statement Segmentation in German Easy Language (StaGE)*, Vienna, Austria. Association for Computational Linguistics.

Buzhou Tang, Jianglu Hu, Xiaolong Wang, and Qingcai Chen. 2018. Recognizing continuous and discontinuous adverse drug reaction mentions from social media using LSTM-CRF. *Wireless Communications and Mobile Computing*, 2018(1):2379208.